The Genesis of Tasso's Narrative Theory

Guercino, *Erminia and the Shepherds*. (Photo courtesy of
The Minneapolis Institute of Arts.)

The Genesis of Tasso's Narrative Theory

English Translations
of the
Early Poetics
and a
Comparative Study
of
Their Significance

Lawrence F. Rhu

Wayne State
University Press
Detroit

Library of Congress Cataloging-in-Publication Data

Rhu, Lawrence F.
   The genesis of Tasso's narrative theory : English translations
of the early poetics and a comparative study of their
significance / Lawrence F. Rhu.
      p.   cm.
   Includes English translations of Torquato Tasso a i lettori,
Discorsi dell'arte poetica, and Allegoria del poema.
   Includes bibliographical references and index.
   ISBN 0-8143-2118-6 (alk. paper).—ISBN 0-8143-2119-4
(pbk. : alk. paper)
   1. Tasso, Torquato, 1544–1595—Influence. 2. Literature,
Comparative—Italian and English. 3. Literature,
Comparative—English and Italian. 4. Poetry—Early works
to 1800. 5. Narrative poetry—History and criticism—Theory,
etc.—Early works to 1800. 6. Ariosto, Lodovico, 1474–1533.
Orlando furioso. 7. Tasso, Torquato, 1544–1595.
Gerusalemme liberata. 8. Spenser, Edmund, 1552?–1599.
Faerie queene. 9. Milton, John, 1608–1674. Paradise lost.
I. Tasso, Torquato, 1544–1595. Torquato Tasso a i lettori.
English. 1993. II. Tasso, Torquato, 1544–1595. Discorsi
dell'arte poetica. English. 1993. III. Tasso, Torquato,
1544–1595. Allegoria del poema. English. 1993.
IV. Title.
PQ4656.R48 1993
851′.4—dc20   92-45872

Designer: Mary Primeau

Cover art: Guercino, *Erminia
and the Shepherds*. (Photo
courtesy of The Minneapolis
Institute of Arts.)

Contents

Preface

This book has two overall aims: to provide readers who do not know Italian with English versions of young Tasso's theoretical writings on narrative poetry and to employ these reflections on epic and romance as tools for reading the poems most relevant to such speculations about the practice of poetry in these genres. With this volume, I thus intend to present readably accurate translations of Tasso's early poetics and to apply them to *Gerusalemme liberata* and to the tradition that Tasso thereby both sought to inherit (especially from Ariosto) and managed to bequeath to his own distinguished heirs, Spenser and Milton.

The contents of the pages that follow include translations of three prose texts by Tasso: his prefatory remarks to the readers of *Rinaldo* (1562), *Discorsi dell'arte poetica* (ca. 1562–65; published in 1587), and "Allegoria del poema" (1575–76), which first appeared in the Bonnà editions of *Gerusalemme liberata* in 1581. The book also contains an ample introductory essay in three parts that attempts to use these theoretical documents as bases for interpreting aspects of both the major Italian poems to which they directly pertain (*Gerusalemme liberata* and *Orlando furioso*) and the major English poems that employ Ariosto and Tasso as exemplary models of narrative art, *The Faerie Queene* and *Paradise Lost*.

There is a need for the translations because these works are the young poet's most relevant obiter dicta about the craft that he succeeded in practicing expertly enough to win our lasting regard. Yet with the exception of Tasso's brief "Allegory" of *Gerusalemme liberata*, they have not been available in English.

The publication in 1973 of an English version of *Discorsi del poema eroico* (which first appeared in Italian in 1594) was a welcome event; but it also complicated matters by tempting critics to read the *Liberata* through the lens of this lengthy treatise; for these later discourses more aptly serve as a gloss upon *Gerusalemme conquistata*, which was initially published in 1593.[1] By that time, Tasso was a battle-scarred veteran of the literary wars that raged over his *Liberata* and *Orlando furioso*; and these poems had become essential touchstones in the ongoing debates between the so-called ancients and moderns. Tasso had significantly altered and expanded his original theorizing in the light of both his polemical exchanges and his extensive revision of the *Liberata*, which transformed it into the *Conquistata*.

But when young Tasso penned *Discorsi dell'arte poetica* in the 1560s, he was fully embarked upon, although he had by no means finished, the journey of the *Liberata*.[2] Later, in the mid-1570s, when he looked back upon his just-completed epic, he asserted that he had intended the early *Discorsi* as a kind of preface or forerunner to that poem; and whether we take him at his word or not, these reflections on the art that Tasso most triumphantly practiced in the *Liberata* undoubtedly bear an integral relation to his chef d'oeuvre.[3] They provide a kind of blueprint to that poem-in-the-making; and, as such, they warrant our most careful attention as readers of the *Liberata*. The other two brief pieces translated here, Tasso's prefatory address to the readers of *Rinaldo* and "Allegoria del poema," are introductory statements that Tasso himself authorized for publication together with his first two narrative poems. Therefore, these two brief pieces and the early *Discorsi* amount to the entire body of narrative theory that Tasso clearly intended for public consumption by the time he had completed the *Liberata*.

However, when Tasso finally published *Discorsi dell'arte poetica* in 1587, he included in the volume with that treatise a selection of letters, most of which were written during 1575–76, when Tasso first brought the *Liberata* to a conclusion. The letters from those two years are extremely interesting and relevant to central questions about Tasso's intentions in his great epic; but their number makes translating all of them a prohibitive task, and the lack of a modern critical edition exacerbates that problem.[4] Originally, I planned to make a selection of them to translate for inclusion in this volume; but the very process of choosing would lead to misrepresentation of Tasso's ambitions.[5] Indeed, when Tasso himself gathered a collection of these letters for the 1587 volume, he was making a decisive gesture of self-representation whose inclusions and exclusions both warrant careful reflection.

In translating Tasso, I have attempted to strike a balance between readability and accuracy. Tasso routinely employs lengthy periods reminiscent of some Latin prose writers, and Italian syntax and inflection carry enough of the memory of such roots and models to enable Italian writers to imitate these ancient examples without undue strain. English writers of the early modern era like Sir Thomas Browne and John Milton were the beneficiaries of a neoclassical culture that encouraged them to follow suit in this regard. However, a modern version of Tasso's Italian prose, such as I have attempted, must sacrifice the amplitude of latinate sentences in the interests of readability, so I have frequently modified Tasso's syntax and broken it down into shorter periods. Other adjustments have been made, and liberties taken, with the same governing motive—the ambition to provide readable and useful renditions of valuable documents for students of Renaissance literature. Although I believe it should go without saying that Tasso's original text constitutes the final authority when it comes to understanding the exact meaning of specific passages and terms and the precise literary concepts that Tasso had in mind, I still think it worth mentioning both here and (via occasional notes) at a few points where I think misprision is especially tempting.[6]

The three-part introductory essay attempts to demonstrate something of the value claimed for these documents in justifying their translation into English. Thus, it constitutes an effort to participate as fully as possible in the ongoing critical conversation about Ariosto, Tasso, Spenser, and Milton, while making special use of relevant perspectives available through familiarity with young Tasso's narrative theory. The texts of his early poetics are, as we say nowadays, "privileged" in this exercise; and I hasten to acknowledge that fact openly from the outset, trusting that their warrant for such favored status will become apparent in what follows.

The first part of the Introduction tries to show the depth of Tasso's involvement both in the neoclassical culture that enabled him to repudiate Ariosto decisively enough to pursue his own ambitions as a poet and in the Counter-Reformation zeitgeist that conditioned his response to the *Furioso*. It also aims to demonstrate how the boundary between the theory and practice of Tasso's art allows more frequent and direct commerce between these domains than is likely to appear without scrutinizing both kinds of documents in tandem. Indeed, this very notion of discursive boundaries in Ariosto and Tasso further pertains to matters of reader response usually associated with the emergence of novelistic fiction in a subsequent era, as I mean to suggest in discussing Ariostan interruptions from Tasso's viewpoint.

The second and third parts of the Introduction entertain problems relevant to students of English and comparative literature and attempt to show points of intersection and divergence between Italian and English traditions of narrative poetry that have been overlooked. For example, I frankly doubt that Spenser had read Tasso's *Discorsi dell'arte poetica* before publishing the first three books of *The Faerie Queene*, although I am confident that he was familiar with "Allegoria del poema," which appeared in the various editions of the *Liberata* that he was likeliest to have known. The Allegory overlaps with previous concerns that vexed Tasso about multiplicity of plot in Ariostan romance and that Aristotelian theory initially enabled him to address. An appreciation of this background helps to render Spenser's Errour (the wood and the monster) legible in a new light; and this viewpoint, in turn, opens a fresh perspective on Milton's figure of Sin and her cosmic neighbor, Chaos. Further, an understanding of Tasso's scruples about authorial intervention and his distinction between epic and tragic heroism puts one in a position to address matters of technique and decorum that have preoccupied Milton's readers from Johnson to Waldock and Fish. When viewed through the perspective of young Tasso's narrative theory, Milton's relationship to both the *Liberata* and the *Furioso* acquires surprising dimensions that seem to have gone undetected heretofore. It is my hope that the Introduction's third part brings these into the open.

Although I completed the greater part of the writing in this book in recent years as a member of the English department at the University of South Carolina, my involvement with the works of Torquato Tasso goes back several decades; and I have incurred significant debts of gratitude for instruction and encouragement that have fostered this project along the way. Judith Kates first guided me to Tasso's *Discorsi dell'arte poetica* when I was a graduate student preparing for general exams. Dante Della Terza and Walter Kaiser oversaw my dissertation, which featured, as an appendix, a previous version of my translation of the *Discorsi*. Maristella Lorch, James Mirollo, and Madison Sowell read and commented upon earlier versions of that translation. To all of them I offer my thanks.

I am also grateful to the Minneapolis Institute of Art, which has allowed me to reproduce the title figure of Guercino's *Erminia and the Shepherds* on this book's cover. For various reasons, numerous critics, both early and late, have seen her as a stand-in for the poet himself. I would not endorse such a view without qualification, but her act of uncovering herself to reveal her identity to the on-looking swain and his children is analogous to my own ambitions in the pages that follow. I hope to bring to the attention of readers without Italian Tasso's early poetics, which contain his narrative theorizing most relevant to *Gerusalemme liberata* and which have often been overlooked because they were not available in English. As Guercino portrays her, Erminia looks much like Minerva, the Roman goddess of wisdom. It is my hope that readers of this book will have more direct access to Tasso's philosophy of art and its applications to his masterwork in the context of the literary tradition that he inherited and decisively influenced.

During the summer of 1990 I took part in the Ariosto-Tasso Institute at Northwestern University, which was sponsored by the National Endowment for the Humanities and both organized and conducted by Albert Ascoli and David Quint. Their guidance of our discussions in Evanston and my conversations with other participants there beneficially influenced my thinking about matters essential to this book. Members of the institute used my translation of *Discorsi dell'arte poetica* as part of the curriculum, and several came forward with useful advice—Ted Cachey and the late Joy Potter in particular. Tom Mayer, whom I met through the institute, provided me with helpful commentary on my introductory essay once it reached completion. There I also met Dennis Looney, who became the most scrupulous reader of my renditions of Tasso's prose and has generously remained available since we broke camp in Evanston. He deserves special thanks.

Daniel Javitch has consistently encouraged my efforts with sensible comments, good humor, and friendship for almost a decade; he thus warrants singling out as a guiding spirit in much of my response to the issues and challenges central to this book. The support and companionship of my wife, Karen, have sustained and delighted me throughout the work on this book, which I dedicate to her as a sign of my gratitude.

Introduction

Authority and Tradition: Young Tasso's Reckoning with Aristotle and Ariosto

Readers of Tasso's *Gerusalemme liberata* would do well to consult his *Discorsi dell'arte poetica* if they want to appreciate some of the young poet's central ambitions in his great epic and to interpret that masterwork in accord with something resembling its author's original intentions. Not long ago, such a claim would have occasioned a skeptical critique from purists then in our midst known as New Critics; and I must hasten to acknowledge my share in their doubts, however unfashionable such an admission has now become in an age of poststructuralism and new historicism. In various ways Tasso's poem—both in its own terms and vis-à-vis certain contingencies, like its place in the literary tradition from Homer to Milton and beyond—far exceeds the explanatory power of the early *Discorsi*. If the notorious intentional fallacy means confining a poem's meanings to its author's perceptible ambitions as they are expressed in extraneous documents like prefatory manifestos, contemporary correspondence, and other such supplementary statements of purpose, let us by all means break those bonds and explore the rich range of options to which sensitive "close reading" of the literary text per se can gain us access.[1]

Confinement, however, comes all too often from the other perspective, when "new critical" purism rules out relevant contexts that locate our responses to a given text in a world of activities that conditioned the production of the work in question. Tasso was one of a number of cinquecento poets (like Trissino, Giraldi, and Pigna) who explored in theory the principles underlying their literary projects. Indeed, as a theorist-poet of the highest order in both callings, Tasso offers us an exceptional opportunity to witness the interplay of two distinctive kinds of discourse that are neither mutually exclusive nor interchangeable. The rare combination of gifts that Tasso employed as a practitioner of both pursuits makes his works exceptionally inviting objects of study. They can afford us the dual perspective of theory and praxis that criticism must normally supply ad hoc wherever it trains its gaze.

We must note, however, that Tasso himself was a purist in matters akin to the scruples of new criticism just cited. In his preface to the readers of *Rinaldo* (1562), Tasso's censure of Ariosto's familiar practice of self-representation in the *Furioso* depends upon a precept from Aristotle's *Poetics*; but it bespeaks an aesthetics as committed to mimetic self-sufficiency in works of narrative art as are Wimsatt and Beardsley's rigorous standards. The plots of such poems should remain uncompromised by extraneous supplements to the ongoing story like Ariosto's moralizing proems. In the same way that new criticism wants texts to stand on their own without external addenda, Tasso wants narration without interference from outside; and speech in the poet's own person constitutes just such a compromise of a poem's representational integrity.

But Tasso here takes Ariostan self-reference to task in terms that are reminiscent of Castiglione's famous manual of conduct for aspiring counselors of princes and kings. Tasso labels Ariosto's habit of speaking in his own person "affectation"—the ultimate outrage against the artful indirection and disguise necessary at court.[2] This subtle reminder of *The Courtier* evokes the aesthetic principle that Castiglione summons to condemn apparent self-consciousness in his ideal counselor of princes: "Ars est celare artem."[3] At court, one should not wear one's art upon one's sleeve, if you will; and it is precisely the open evidence of the poet's manipulation of his story that troubles Tasso about the *Furioso*. Yet he responds to this apparently aesthetic blemish in a manner marked by the values of a social institution; and the exception he takes to Ariosto's artistry thus reveals the contaminating influence of "extraneous" concerns despite its ostensible origins in a purely theoretical consideration.

Thus, Tasso's early *Discorsi* are not only a telling gloss upon the *Liberata* that demonstrates the principles of composition governing many of his crucial choices as a literary artist of the highest accomplishment; they also reveal his involvement in courtly politics and patronage, the book market, and institutional religion. His youthful opinion about a routine feature in *Orlando furioso* both prominent and frequent enough to occasion inevitable notice invites speculation and inference beyond the aesthetic issues that Tasso's critique apparently addresses while nonetheless signaling the undeniable importance of those very concerns. In many ways Ariosto's popular poem had itself become an institution, fully authorized by the prevailing values of mid-cinquecento classicism despite their sometimes questionable applicability to the text itself. As Daniel Javitch has demonstrated, the *Furioso* was assimilated to changed cultural circumstances as much by fiat and arbitrary intervention as by its suitably fitting the new standards that had emerged.[4] Due to Ariosto's role as the reigning laureate in modern Italy, Tasso's response to his best-selling precursor was the most crucial reckoning required of him by his culture; however, the necessity of that reckoning also gave Tasso the chance to distinguish himself as the creator of an epic alternative according to post-Ariostan criteria derived from the widespread circulation of Aristotle's *Poetics*.

The revival of interest in that brief treatise on aesthetics pervaded the literary milieu in which Tasso came of age as both a poet and theorist. As Baxter Hathaway points out, no such attention to Aristotle as a literary theorist preoccupied the Italian world of letters prior to Ariosto's death in 1533, despite the rediscovery of the *Poetics* three-and-a-half decades earlier; but through the publication of Alessandro de' Pazzi's Latin translation of that text in 1536, it began to gain widespread currency.[5] Although Aristotle himself had focused primarily upon principles of composition in tragic drama, his ideas were promptly absorbed into both the discussion of narrative theory and the production of narrative poems, which the popularity of *Orlando furioso* had made fashionable among the literati.

Tasso's father struggled unsuccessfully to adapt himself to

17

this new dispensation in his own effort to rival Ariosto, *L'Amadigi*, published in 1560; and the other notable failure among the heroic poems that intervened between the *Furioso* and the *Liberata*, Trissino's *Italia liberata da'i goti* (published in 1547), was composed by a theorist-poet who supplemented the original four "divisions" of his *Poetica* (published in 1529) with two new ones in 1562 that bear the strong impress of Aristotle's brief treatise. The middle decades of the century also saw the publication of a spate of significant commentaries on the *Poetics*; between 1548 and 1560 Robortello, Lombardi and Maggi, and Vettori provided sustained expositions of Aristotle's literary theory that further testify to its cultural centrality during the years in which Tasso's sensibility as a poet and theorist initially took shape.[6] Although neo-Aristotelian theory had merged in many ways with Horatian precepts and although Tasso himself expressed reservations about uncompromising orthodoxy in this regard, his early poetics are undeniably the product of a rigorous appeal to Aristotle's legitimating power among midcentury literati.[7]

The degree to which this influence permeates young Tasso's efforts as a poet and theorist requires prompt acknowledgment if we wish fully to appreciate the interaction between his literary efforts and his cultural environment. In fact, if we remember that Tasso's own teacher in Padova, Sperone Speroni, accused his star pupil of plagiarism, we can see that these issues crystallized early and vividly in this poet's career.[8] Speroni was the primary arbiter of neoclassical orthodoxy in young Tasso's eyes and virtually his guru in matters of literary theory, as the conclusion of the first discourse in *Discorsi dell'arte poetica* makes clear. Tasso shifts from speculation to autobiography when he describes his visits to Speroni's study which "seemed to [him] a replica of that Academy and Lyceum where the Socratic and Platonic philosophers used to hold their discussions." But if we were to ask that prestigious scholar, "Who wrote *Discorsi dell'arte poetica*?," ours would not be an idle question; nor would it receive a conventional answer. Speroni's accusation fits in with a pattern of academic backbiting and jealousy most notably reminiscent of similar charges traded by Tasso's chief rivals in the debate over unity of plot central to the early *Discorsi*, namely, Giraldi and Pigna, whose defenses of Ariostan romance were both published in 1554.[9] Like Tasso and Speroni, they were teacher and pupil; and evidently enough intellectual cross-fertilization had occurred between them to make each suspicious of the other's appropriations of his ideas.

But the exchange of ideas between Tasso and Speroni took place in different terms and with different priorities, since both their agendas were set by strong classicizing tendencies. The baldest sort of evidence for this can be found in the prose and poetry that Tasso produced early in his career; for at times he seems merely a ventriloquist or even a self-serving name-dropper, and it is Aristotle and Homer whose words he mouths or manner of composition he conspicuously displays. The obviousness of such echoes may dampen our enthusiasm for Tasso's artistry if we bring to these passages the usual expectation of some sort of personal stylistic distinction and demonstrable originality even in imitative reprises of ancient texts. For example, prior familiarity with Tasso's breathtakingly purple passage on the parallel unity of the cosmos and the perfect heroic poem, which thus assimilates the poet to God the creator, could make the heart sink of a reader who came upon this hardly thrilling excerpt from the same text: "Wholeness will be found in the plot if it has a beginning, a middle, and an end. The beginning is that which, by necessity, comes after nothing else; the other things come after it. The end is that which comes after the other things; nothing comes after it. The middle is situated between the beginning and the end; and it comes after some things and some things come after it." Perhaps Speroni thought he had said that and was outraged to find it in a manuscript circulated under Tasso's name, and perhaps Tasso thought he wrote it himself. But it is patently an unacknowledged citation from Aristotle's *Poetics*.[10]

Furthermore, I am confident that a writer as skillful as Tasso would probably never have said anything that silly unless, in some way, he felt he had to. The coercive pressure that Tasso experienced in this regard was not necessarily conscious but, rather, a reflex occasioned at a critical turn in his argument when

an automatic appeal to first principles seemed required. His statement of the obvious pales beside the rhetorical tour de force that
he managed in full awareness of the high stakes at issue when he
formulated his version of the basic axiom of *discordia concors*;
but his mechanical citation of Aristotle reveals the foundations
not of his own thought alone but of the cultural movement in
which he participated. Clichés, by their very nature, require
widespread collaboration; and Tasso's voice emerges from a
crowd of like-minded adherents to the new classicism sponsored
by the mid-cinquecento reception of Aristotle's *Poetics*. Tasso
himself uses the most extravagant terms to pledge allegiance to
the absolute authority of Aristotelian precepts in his early
Discorsi. He simply asserts that Aristotle knew everything that
could matter about the question at hand: "There is surely no
poetic genre today in use, nor was there such in ancient times,
nor will such arise in a long cycle of centuries, that Aristotle did
not fathom."[11]

The prominent positioning of Homeric allusions in the *Liberata* bespeaks a kindred process of giving pride of place to notably
authoritative pre-texts; for the ascendency of the *Poetics* entails
the concomitant rise in the stock of those texts which it endorses
as exemplary. Also, the less mediated such imitative reprises
appear, the more evidence we have for their capacity to mark a
new poem with a canonical stamp of approval by openly affiliat-
ing it with an esteemed ancient lineage. Tasso patently wants his
poem to sound Homeric, as both the obviousness of such echoes
indicates and their location in the foreground of his epic con-
firms; and Aristotle provides the prime motive for ambitions of
this sort, because he regularly uses the *Iliad* and the *Odyssey* to
exemplify the principles of composition that he prescribes.[12]

The muster of the Christian forces in the *Liberata*'s first
canto recalls the catalogue of ships in the *Iliad*'s second book
both in its substance and in the preliminary invocation by which
Tasso summons the muse on this occasion. This appeal for divine favor is the second such traditional call for inspiration in
the opening thirty-six octaves of his poem; in what remains of
the entire epic, there will only be three more instances of this
ancient protocol. Likewise, in canto 3 Erminia stands atop the

walls of Jerusalem and reviews the assembled Crusade, identify-
ing its leaders for Aladino in a manner directly reminiscent of
Helen's scene of *teichoskopia* in the *Iliad*'s third book. The
baldness of such references is especially striking, as is their being clustered so close to the poem's beginning. These features of
Tasso's early Homeric citations advertise unforgettably the gene-
alogy he wants to claim for the *Liberata*.

In the early *Discorsi* Tasso dismisses, as extraneous imposi-
tions upon a literary text, what sound suspiciously like the sort
of marginal glosses and editorial commentaries that Venetian
publishers used to promote *Orlando furioso*. He condemns as
"imperfect" poems whose disorderly plots require them to "go
a-begging elsewhere extra aids to understanding" and adds that
"one can perhaps criticize this fault in certain modern poems
where one needs to resort to prefatory prose explanations—for
whatever clarity is gained by prose arguments and other such
devices is neither artful nor truly poetic; it is extrinsic and unearned."[13] In censuring such paratextual apparatuses for their
lack of integral connection to the poem-in-progress, Tasso con-
tinues the line of argument that he originally broached in his
preface to *Rinaldo*. In the name of Aristotle, he there took
Ariosto to task for speaking in his own voice in his poem, rather
than exclusively practicing, as the *Poetics* prescribes, the imitation of the action that he chose to relate. Homer's famous repu-
tation for anonymity derives from this Aristotelian principle;
and Tasso tenaciously adhered to it, virtually banishing himself
from the precincts of his own poem in the process. However, in
ways other than direct address, Tasso makes his intentions felt
and signals his participation in the strict classicizing trends of his
cultural moment, as the unmistakably Homeric reprises in the
foreground of his epic boldly announce.

In his *Comparazione di Homero, Virgilio, e Torquato* of
1607, Paolo Beni pointed out the Homeric lineage of the ambas-
sadors to Goffredo in the second half of canto 2 of the *Liberata*.[14] His perception of the Achillean ancestry of Argante's
rage and the Odyssean origins of Alete's eloquent dissembling
makes this passage nicely cohere with the broader strokes of imitation in the surrounding cantos that almost single themselves

21

out. Further, a reckoning with Argante in this regard can refine one's sense of the overall Iliadic shape of Tasso's plot; for in that broad perspective upon the poem's basic structure, Rinaldo is certainly the Achilles figure whose withdrawal from battle prolongs the siege of Jerusalem and whose return makes victory possible. But the mania characteristic of the Greek hero and thematically central to Homer's epic is strategically displaced, in its full manifestation, onto Argante. This transfer of Achilles' excessive wrath to the pagan warrior makes the Christian recuperation of Rinaldo more credible and easier to effect, since his own outrage consequently remains within the manageable bounds of contrition and penance. Achilles, the ephebic antagonist of Apollo himself, imparts a legacy too dangerous for the Christian hero to inherit without modification. Thus, Tasso skillfully adjusts his options to meet the needs of his poem's ideological limits.[15]

But I want to make a less subtle point about Tasso's artistry and the authoritative discourses that impinge upon it, for these pressures sometimes make themselves felt *grosso modo*. I mean neither to deny the refinements of Tasso's poetry nor to neglect the delicate refashioning of traditions that he often achieved.[16] He aimed, from early in his career, to chart a middle course between extremes that invited his participation in their more radical commitments. Tasso indicated in the preface to *Rinaldo* that he wanted to eschew reductive evaluation both by the severe followers of Aristotle and by those overly enamored of Ariosto.[17] When he was completing the *Liberata* in the mid-1570s, he was similarly wary of the strict neoclassicism characteristic of those he tellingly dubbed the *Castelvetrici*, while he nonetheless aimed to satisfy certain of their basic principles.[18] Actually, what happened to Tasso's epic in the long run of its early modern reception demonstrates a text's vulnerability to the crudest claims of its cultural moment; for together with the *Furioso*, the *Liberata* became the site of a prolonged quarrel between the so-called ancients and moderns. The polemical postures in this debate frequently encouraged an extreme binarism that inevitably blurred the discriminating choices that went into the composition of Tasso's chef d'oeuvre. But Tasso himself was very much susceptible to such pressures before they emerged in the critical wrangling over his poem.

If we turn to Armida's change of heart near the poem's close, we can examine a crucial juncture in the plot where major ideological demands converged upon the poet and where criticism has found recurrent cause to review and debate Tasso's choices. The suddenness of this Circean temptress's transformation often bothers readers, as does the scriptural citation that accompanies it. Maurice Bowra attempts to defend Tasso at this turn in his plot by contextualizing the abrupt alteration of her character; sudden conversions, it seems, were by no means rare occurrences in the annals of Counter-Reformation Italy.[19] Likewise, Walter Stephens tries to defend Tasso by unearthing the literary history behind the telegraphically scriptural phrasing of Armida's surrender to Rinaldo:

> "Ecco l'ancilla tua; d'essa a tuo senno
> dispon," gli disse, "e le fia legge il cenno."
> (20.136.7–8)[20]

> "Behold your handmaid; dispose of her at your discretion," she
> said, "and your command shall be her law."

This bald citation of the Virgin's acceptance of Gabriel's annunciation of her maternal role in the new dispensation had been previously appropriated by Petrarch and strategically employed in secular literature. According to Stephens, critics who deplore the "too obvious echoes" in Armida's notorious line miss the subtler allusions to relevant intertexts that mediate between Tasso and the Gospel speech.[21]

Unfortunately, both Bowra and Stephens fail to refer to Tasso's own misgivings about this passage as he recorded them in a letter of July 1575 to Scipione Gonzaga, one of the *revisori* whom the poet consulted during the final drafting of the *Liberata*;[22] for the suddenness of Armida's change of heart also bothered Tasso, and neither contemporary religious practice nor intertextual recall appeased his concerns, though both may help us to explain his anxieties in this regard. The perfunctory Aristotelianism that I mentioned earlier does not directly apply to

23

Armida, because it focuses on wholeness of plot, which requires a beginning, a middle, and an end. But the principle of wholeness itself transfers usefully to the problems a modern reader might experience about her as a fictional character; for her change of heart seems inadequately motivated, since she undergoes no intermediate stage between intransigence and submission. Her character has no middle. The formal realism of modern fiction has ambitions akin to those of Aristotelian mimesis and to the impulses that made Tasso insist upon basing his epic upon historical grounds.[23] Thus, Armida's absent middle, the gap in her psychological development, could understandably have given Tasso pause. However, character itself in the *Liberata* is as much premised upon ancient models as upon detailed representation; hence, the expectation of psychological wholeness of character is premature, though we are witnessing a significant stage in the evolution toward the legitimate application of such principles of criticism. Tasso's misgivings about Armida's abrupt transformation reflect a step along this path toward psychological realism.

But Tasso also expressed a reluctance to employ biblical stories as a basis for poetic creation because tenets of faith frequently derived from them. The adjustments that a poet might want to work upon the raw material of his story would be inhibited by the sacredness of such sources, and he would thus have to surrender his freedom to invent.[24] Armida, of course, borrows only a line from the Gospel; but its fame makes this echo as blatant as any citation in the entire *Liberata*. Further, the relocation of the Virgin's line into this context is frankly quite shocking if we reflect upon some of its possible implications. Joseph's misdeeming thoughts, for example, find a secure ground if you are fresh from a visit to Armida's palace; the Blessed Mother, it seems, has a torrid past. Such associations are unsettling once we begin making them with an awareness of the kind of religious scrupulosity that compelled Tasso enough to prompt him "voluntarily" both to visit representatives of the Inquisition and to submit his masterwork to the critical perusal of a reader evidently as undiscerning as the powerful cleric, Silvio Antoniano, whose ecclesiatical clout could smooth the way for the *Liberata*'s uncensored publication.[25] Delicate Petrarchan effects were simply inaudible in such quarters, where dogmatic religiosity held sway. Despite Tasso's notable skills as an author, his writings, like his psyche, were fatefully susceptible to authorities like these at large in his age. They left their mark upon the composition of his poem both where he resisted them and where he gave them their way.

In the first discourse in *Discorsi dell'arte poetica* Tasso aims to found heroic poetry's truth firmly upon religious faith and historical records; for these are the basic authorities that he can discern through a reckoning with the literary tradition that he means to inherit and the critical and confessional sanctions of his present moment. Premised upon both these authorities, an epic's foundations are secure; and its power to gain conviction in the response of its readers is likewise dependable. As the only convert whose experience of that spiritual transformation is detailed within Tasso's poem, Clorinda dramatizes the process by which true religion ultimately wins interior assent despite strong motives for the stiffest resistance; and she passes through aspects of her change of heart in a manner that directly evokes the language and themes of the first of Tasso's early *Discorsi*. Her spiritual ordeal thus parallels the reader's experience of modern epic, as Tasso conceives it; and the change that she goes through can therefore provide telling analogues for understanding problems in both the composition and the interpretation of *Gerusalemme liberata*.

Clorinda enters the poem on an occasion where lying is an honorable activity. When she arrives in Jerusalem, Sofronia is bravely accepting a martyr's death at the stake for fabricating a tale of her responsibility in the disappearance of the stolen image of the Virgin from Aladino's mosque, where Ismeno had been practicing demonic enchantments upon it. Sofronia's false confession will save the rest of the Christian minority within the walls of Jerusalem and thus amounts to a grand gesture of charity:

> Magnanima menzogna, or quand' è il vero
> sí bello che si possa a te preporre?
> (2.22.3–4)

O noble lie, now when is truth so beautiful that it can be preferred to you?

Olindo joins Sofronia in this sacrifice; and her role as his beloved seems to have the metamorphic power of the neo-Platonic object of desire, as well as the inspirational solace of Christian counsel, reflecting a standard Renaissance fusion of these diverse traditions. Sofronia endeavors to change Olindo's erotic ardor into a passion for virtue and, ultimately, into devotion to the summum bonum itself and to transform his originally amatory motives into an appetite for martyrdom:

> Amico, altri pensieri, altri lamenti,
> per piú alta cagione il tempo chiede.
> Ché non pensi a tue colpe? e non rammenti
> qual Dio prometta a i buoni ampia mercede?
> Soffri in suo nome, e fian dolci i tormenti,
> e lieto aspira a la superna sede.
> Mira 'l ciel com'è bello, e mira il sole
> ch'a sé par che n'inviti e ne console.
>
> (2.36)

My friend, the time requires other thoughts, other laments, for loftier reason. Why are you not thinking upon your sins and calling to mind what ample reward God promises the righteous? Suffer in his name and your torments will become blessed; and gladly aspire to your heavenly station. Behold the sky how beautiful it is, and behold the sun how it comforts us and seems to invite us there.

Recognized by the tigress crest on her helmet, Clorinda brings this woeful pageant to a halt by her intervention. She is most moved by Sofronia, the potential martyr whose demeanor describes Clorinda's own destiny ten cantos later:

> E tacer lei con gli occhi al ciel sí fisa
> ch'anzi 'l morir par di qua giú divisa.
>
> (2.42.7–8)

And she remains silent, with her eyes so fixed on the sky that she seems before death to be separated from down here.

26

The king grants Clorinda's request to spare the condemned, in anticipation of her services to be rendered for the city under siege. But she also solves the crime; or, at least, she explains the event that occasioned the spectacle under way upon her arrival. Strikingly, her rationale for the disappearance of the image reflects Tasso's own scrupulosity about precision in religious observance, whereas, ironically, Ismeno, who is also a convert (though to a false religion), has been breaking Muslim law in his ignorance while doing willful violence to a sacred Christian image. But Clorinda's clarifying perception constitutes an example of what we may fairly call the Islamic marvelous that mirrors the poet's trust in Christian grounds for credible miracles in a modern epic.

> Fu de le nostre leggi irriverenza
> quell'opra far che persuase il mago:
> ché non convien ne' nostri tèmpi a nui
> gl'idoli avere, e men gl'idoli altrui.
>
> Dunque suso a Macon recar mi giova
> il miracol de l'opra, ed ei la fece
> per dimostrar ch'i tèmpi sui con nova
> religion contaminar non lece.
> (2.50.5–51.4)

> It was lack of reverence for our laws to do that work that the wizard persuaded you to, for it is not proper for us to have images in our temples, and even less the images of others. Therefore it pleases me to refer the miracle of the deed to Mahoun above; and he did it to demonstrate that it is not permitted to pollute his temples with an alien religion.

If it is *nova religion* that contaminates the mosque and thus causes Muhammad on high to intercede, the adjective here indicates the strangeness of alien belief, rather than its temporal newness; for Christianity, of course, is prior to Islam. Tasso's effort to inherit classical literary forms involved him in a similar transaction with what he called the "Gentile" religion of pagandom; and he stresses the modern poet's need to purge epic's traditional divine machinery of such heathen influences.[26] Trissino's failure fully to make this adjustment exemplifies the incomplete appropriation of classical forms, since vestiges of Greco-Roman religion remain in his *Italia liberata da'i goti* despite its patently Christian sympathies.[27] Tasso seeks entirely to empty of their pagan associations inherited precedents for otherworldly intervention and to replenish them with acceptable referents.[28]

Clorinda is a stickler for precision in details of a similar kind; however, both for her and for Tasso, the value of religious truth becomes confused with rhetorical efficacy. She repeats an argument of Tasso's from the *Discorsi* to defend her persistence in allegiance to Islam when Arsete fills in the background of her mother's injunction that she be baptized a Christian and urges her to act upon it. Clorinda initially rejects the possibility of conversion to the ideologically correct position in Tasso's scheme of things on the very same grounds that he claims will assure belief in epic marvels founded upon true religion; for Tasso asserts in his early poetics that an opinion imbibed in the cradle along with one's milk is an effective basis for gaining credit for a particular belief:

> These same works, if attention is given to the virtue and power that have wrought them, are deemed verisimilar. Since our people have imbibed this opinion in the cradle, along with their milk, . . . it does not appear to them beyond verisimilitude. Indeed, they not only believe it possible but think it has happened many times and can happen many times again.[29]

Clorinda employs the same premise to reject Arsete's importuning her not to do battle against the Christians and to affirm her faith in Islam:

> Rasserenando il volto, al fin gli dice:
> "Quella fé seguirò che vera or parmi,
> *che tu co'l latte già de la nutrice*
> *sugger mi fèsti* e che vuoi dubbia or farmi;
> né per temenza lascierò, né lice
> a magnanimo cor, l'impresa e l'armi,
> non se la morte nel piú fer sembiante
> che sgomenti i mortali avessi inante."
> (12.41, emphasis mine)

28

Clearing her countenance, at last she says to him: "I shall follow that faith that seems to me true at this moment, that once you caused me to drink in with my nurse's milk, and that now you wish to make me doubtful of. Nor shall I abandon out of fear (nor is that permitted the magnanimous heart) my enterprise and my weapons: not if I had before me Death in the fearfullest shape in which he terrifies mortal men."

The language of Clorinda's self-justification here echoes Tasso's description of Sofronia's magnanimous willingness to suffer martyrdom at the stake on behalf of her coreligionists. More importantly, Clorinda's rationale for her conduct repeats Tasso's line of reasoning for the persuasive power of epic marvels founded upon Christian faith; for this potentially mistaken martyr here falls into a trap akin to the one Tasso openly sets for his readers at the start of his poem. There he executes a reprise of the Epicurean topos employed in *The Courtier* to justify a devotion to self-cultivation because of its utility for the commonweal (a topos also used by his father, it is worth noting, in *L'Amadigi*, when he defends the pleasures of that text).[30] But in Clorinda's case, such altruism risks hell's fire, which is a very present danger; and while Tasso's earnest plea for heaven's pardon of his practice of embroidering the truth with seductive delights bespeaks an ebbing confidence in the courtier's stratagem of salutary deception, his emphasis on the expressive power of true religion dangerously subordinates the value of truth to the efficacy of linguistic ploys. True religion becomes merely useful to the poet—a condition of the credit that he wishes to obtain with his readers, not an essential value independent of rhetorical performance.

Fortunately for Clorinda, she misremembers who nursed her; and this oversight enables the careful reader to savor the subtlety of Tasso's dramatic irony in the passage just cited. For we learn from Arsete that Clorinda's mother denied her the milk from her breast (12.27.5–6); and his tale of the tigress who scared him up a tree during his escape from Ethiopia with the infant Clorinda informs us that that apparently ferocious beast turned out to be surprisingly mild and suckled his charge, whom he had abandoned in fright. The symbol on Clorinda's helmet crest thus betokens a prior claim upon her; and what *seems* true to her is, in fact, false. But the courtier-poet's involvement with the manipulation of appearances continually threatens to remove from beneath his poem the secure footing upon which he ultimately means it to stand. The lost innocence of unfeigned honesty is irrecoverable; and "the truest poetry" becomes, in Touchstone's phrase, "the most feigning" (*As You Like It* 3.3.16).[31] However, this is the world not only of Shakespeare's Orlando but also of Ariosto's Orlando—and of his Saint John, as well. The urgency of Tasso's drive for sound bases for epic composition in history and Christianity could not allow him to accept Touchstone's proposition; but the process of poetic representation itself entangles truth in partiality and indirection, disabling the absolute claims that Tasso wants to make for it and requiring pardon from the professed source of his inspiration.

Clorinda's conversion distinguishes her among the heroines of the *Liberata*; she is the only convert among them, although the other two seem to be heading more or less in that same direction by the poem's end. That inclination, or the fait accompli, is Tasso's means of restoring these exceptionally attractive figures to the side of the angels in the ideological system of his epic; and failure to do so would wreak further havoc upon the rigid binarism that overtly defines good and evil in his poem's moral universe. Just as the rhetoric of deception's close ties with the dominant truth values of history and religion in the *Liberata* dangerously qualify their claims upon our convictions, the emotional appeal of its heathen women threatens to topple the structures of belief that the poem ostensibly endorses. These outlaws win hearts despite obviously good reasons to counter that flow of feeling; and Tasso wisely reforms them or, at least, shows enough signs of doing so to keep their personal charisma from compromising his overall designs.

Clorinda's suckling at the dugs of a tigress notably departs from the pattern available to Tasso in the likliest Virgilian model for a woman warrior, Camilla, who was thus nourished by a wild mare.

30

Hic natam in dumis interque horrentia lustra
armentalis equae mammis et lacte ferino
nutribat teneris immulgens ubera labris
(*Aeneid* 11.570–72)[32]

Here in undergrowth
Amid rough haunts of beasts he nursed his daughter
Putting her to the breasts of a wild mare
Whose teats he milked into her tender mouth.

Rather, the infant Clorinda's feral pap metaphorically affiliates
her with the two most prominent Christian heroes in Tasso's
poem, Goffredo and Rinaldo, both of whom seem to certain
others to demonstrate the qualities that the influence of such
bestial nurture could promote. The presence of this motif in
their stories also indicates their derivation from a Virgilian
model—Aeneas' abandonment of Dido and the denunciation
that she delivers to him as he takes his leave. Of course, it
comes as no surprise to hear that Goffredo is based upon the
hero of Virgil's poem; but Tasso manages a deft association of
Goffredo's better judgment in the matter of Armida, with
Rinaldo's finally seeing the light in this regard. When the jilted
Armida bitterly denies Rinaldo's human origins, she directly
echoes the fierce repudiation that Dido makes of Aeneas' ostensible humanity, as an examination of the two passages clearly
reveals:

Nec tibi diva parens, generis nec Dardanus auctor,
perfide; sed duris genuit te cautibus horrens
Caucasus, Hyrcanaeque admorunt ubera tigres.
nam quid dissimulo? aut quae me ad maiora reservo?
num fletu ingemuit nostro? num lumina flexit?
num lacrimas victus dedit aut miseratus amantem est?
(*Aeneid* 4.365–70)

No goddess was your mother. Dardanus
Was not the founder of your family.
Liar and cheat! Some rough Caucasian cliff
Begot you on flint. Hyrcanian tigresses

Tendered their teats to you. Why should I palter?
Why still hold back for more indignity?
Sigh, did he, while I wept? Or look at me?
Or yield a tear, or pity her who loved him?

Né te Sofia produsse e non sei nato
de l'azio sangue tu; te l'onda insana
del mar produsse e 'l Caucaso gelato,
e le mamme allattàr di tigre ircana.
Che dissimulo io piú? l'uomo spietato
pur un segno non diè di mente umana.
Forse cambiò color? forse al mio duolo
bagnò almen gli occhi o sparse un sospir solo?
                                        (16.57)

Sophia did not give birth to you, and you are
not born of the blood of the Azzi; the raging
ocean wave and frozen Caucasus gave birth to you,
and the dugs of the Hyrcanian tigress gave you
milk. Why do I pretend any longer? The heartless
man gave not a single sign of human emotion. Did
he change color, perhaps? did he at least for my
sorrow bathe his eyes, perhaps, or drop a single
sigh?

Armida's bitter outcry at this juncture recalls the terms in
which the smitten crusaders who were originally keen to assist
the enchantress ruminated upon Goffredo's potential resistance
of her moving appeal for their aid:

Se mercé da Goffredo or non impetra
ben fu rabbiosa tigre a lui nutrice,
e 'l produsse in aspr'alpe orrida pietra
o l'onda che nel mar si frange e spuma:
crudel, che tal beltà turba e consuma.
                                        (4.77.4–8)

If she does not get aid from Godfrey now, surely a raging tigress
was his nurse and among rugged mountains the forbidding rock
ridge brought him forth, or the wave that shatters itself and froths
in the sea: cruel man, that distresses and destroys such beauty.

32

This recollection nicely assimilates the temperament of the Christian captain to that of his right-hand man, once he has begun to realize the errors of his ways. But Tasso's method of introducing Clorinda into this system of spiritual kinship involves an equally deft gesture of the imagination; for it entails a narrative elaboration of the figurative terms employed to denigrate the exemplary heroes of the Crusade at moments when they most emphatically demonstrate their allegiance to the Christian cause despite compelling temptations to the contrary. The hard choices they feel obliged to make require a seemingly inhuman resistance and thus occasion bitter observations to this effect; but in Clorinda's case, Tasso materializes the disparaging metaphors by providing her with the appropriate beast for her nurse in the past. In Arsete's tale of their flight from Ethiopia, the inclusion of a tigress who gives the infant suck and thereby administers saving nourishment at the crucial moment assures Clorinda's predisposition to believe in the creed that she fights until the final moment of her life.

Tasso excluded biblical stories as source material for epic plots because tenets of faith may depend upon them.[33] However, indirect allusions to the Gospel seem permissible even though imaginative tampering in explicit ways with scriptural tales of doctrinal consequence was taboo. We can deduce such an allowance through this conversion narrative's connection, via the Ethiopian eunuch Arsete, to the story in Acts 8 about the apostle Philip. According to the New Testament account, his explication of an excerpt from the fourth Servant Song in Isaiah 53 occasions the baptism of a eunuch who served the Ethiopian queen Candace. In Clorinda's experience it is Arsete who, despite his previously neglected promise to her mother to baptize her daughter, provides a timely reminder of her destined devotion to the Christian faith. Likewise, although both he and Clorinda perhaps miss the point of his recollection, he tells the tale that makes clear that the nourishment she imbibed as an infant in his charge did not preclude her salvation. The tigress interceded with vital sustenance indeed, although both human parties to that adventure remain in the dark about its ultimate implications.

33

David Quint, who suggested to me the link between Arsete and Philip's Ethiopian convert, has tellingly elaborated the historical context of Counter-Reformation contacts with Coptic Christians as they bear upon this moment in the *Liberata*.[34] But what concerns me here is the theoretical context and how issues broached by Tasso in his early *Discorsi* are elaborated in his narrative practice. Clorinda's drama of belief relates directly to the issue of verisimilitude because, just as her experience amounts to a transformation of Virgil's metaphor into an episode in a story, it likewise turns the logic of Tasso's poetics about what makes things seem true into a narrative event. In doing so, Clorinda's agon comes fully to participate in the profound ambivalence about signs and their meanings characteristic of Tasso's art and his aesthetics. Veracity is not verisimilitude; but once the value of truth yields to the needs of rhetorical efficacy, this distinction can easily get lost. The authoritative grounds of truth (which, for Tasso, are history and Christian religion) become subject to regular adjustments depending on their impact upon the audience. Since what makes something believable can differ notably from what makes something true, Tasso drifts in the treacherous waters between these two poles, continually in danger of losing sight of his point of departure and his guiding principles. Does Clorinda convert merely because of her earliest conditioning? Can the dramatic irony of her predisposition to Christianity be reduced to the circumstances of her infantile experience, which make her, quite literally, a "sucker" for such an option?

The scene of Clorinda's complete turn to the light of true religion indicates its literary design in a notable way that explicitly affiliates it with classical precursors while embodying Christian values; for this dramatic scene of conversion contains a recognition scene that plainly calls itself by name. The main pretext for this episode in Clorinda's story is Boiardo's description of the duel between Orlando and Agricane that concludes with the baptism of the penitent pagan as he is dying from wounds inflicted by the minister of that saving last rite.[35] Tancredi per-

34

forms the same service for Clorinda, but Tasso structures his version of this episode with a theoretical self-consciousness that he betrays by virtually labeling its Aristotelian features. The language in his descriptive response to this action merges with the terminology of his poetics of representation—one of whose key precepts insists upon mimesis without authorial commentary and thus seems to disallow even this fugitive sort of glossing. This aside in the poet's own voice is notably brief and urgent; and it corresponds to the practice in Homer and Virgil of succinct apostrophes from the poet to his heroes, especially at moments of high emotion. Nonetheless, the terms of Tasso's outburst amount to an irrepressible revelation of the poet's shaping influence upon a text that he usually prefers to let stand completely free from such signs of his own presence:

> Tremar sentí la man, mentre la fronte
> non conosciuta ancor sciolse e scoprio.
> La vide, conobbe, e restò senza
> e voce e moto. Ahi vista! Ahi conoscenza!
> (12.67.5–8)

He felt his hand tremble while it freed and revealed the face as yet unknown. He saw it. He knew it. And remained without voice or motion. Alas the sight! alas the recognition![36]

The crescendo of variations on the same verbal root in three successive lines—*conosciuta, conobbe, conoscenza*—culminates in an announcement of the type of scene that we here behold. Tasso thus explicitly displays his poem's fulfillment of structural requirements that he elaborates in his *Discorsi*, although doing so any more openly would amount to a violation of the very source of the poetic principle that he here seeks to put into practice.

This interior tagging of an episode signals that it measures up to the canons of Aristotelian orthodoxy and thus advertizes discreetly that Tasso's epic contains a recognition scene typical of the complex plots described in the *Poetics*. Such indirect self-promotion bespeaks the courtier's manner of bidding for preferment without revealing personal ambition; but this oblique gloss

35

also accomplishes a purpose similar to that of many commentaries and paratexts attached by profit-seeking publishers to their editions of *Orlando furioso*. Tasso's neoclassical poetics are an index of changing values due to the mid-cinquecento circulation of Aristotle's treatise and the assimilation of its standards by a significant portion of the literati. Their new classicism occasioned a widespread revamping of the very idea of the *Furioso* itself, for savvy men of the press reissued that text with supplementary matter that affiliated it with distinguished precursors from the ancient tradition and thus provided it with an impressive pedigree.[37] Young Tasso dismisses editions of this sort as crudely encumbered by external addenda that actually betray the shortcomings of their inherent artistry, and this critical censure merely extends the same principle operative in his citation of Aristotle's caveat against a poet's speaking in his own voice. But Tasso himself devises means to incorporate the language of his literary theorizing within the bounds of his poetic performance; and he thus achieves similar effects while disclaiming participation in such stratagems, whose open practice his poetics roundly disparages, as does the manual of courtly etiquette that he particularly esteemed.[38]

The intimate bond between theory and practice in Tasso's approach to his art makes their separation into distinctive fields of discourse a precarious exercise in categorical precision. Undeniably, Tasso differentiated between them and thus had to stage their fusion with all due propriety; but anyone familiar with the early poetics can hear the lexicon of Tasso's narrative theory emerging in his depiction of the events of the First Crusade. For example, when Goffredo first addresses his fellow leaders in the opening canto, his language is laden with key terms from Tasso's poetics:

Turchi, Persi, Antiochia (*illustre* suono
e di nome *magnifico* e di cose)
opre nostre non già, ma del Ciel dono
furo, e vittorie fur *meravigliose*.
Or se da noi rivolte e torte sono
contro quel fin che 'l donator *dispose*,

36

temo ce 'n privi, e *favola* a le genti
quel sí *chiaro* rimbombo al fin diventi.
                    (1.26, emphasis mine)

> The Turks, the Persians, Antioch (a noble list, redoubtable both
> for the names and for the deeds)—they were not at all our doing,
> but Heaven's gift, and marvellous victories they were. Now if by
> us they are twisted and turned contrary to the ends that the Giver
> intended, I fear lest he take them from us, and lest so famous a
> report should come at last to be a fable for the nations.

My italics merely accent the obvious words that frequently occur
in the early *Discorsi*. Teleological pressure or, if you will, a providential sense of an ending haunts this inaugural address, as well;
it is audible in the repeated word *fin*. This proleptic eye on the
crusaders' ultimate goal—and the poem's conclusion—bespeaks
Tasso's fundamental apprehension about Ariostan romance,
whose potentially interminable production of further episodes
occasioned his most anxious speculations.[39] Thus, Tasso's recourse in the next stanza to the language of *entrelacement* typical
of the *Furioso* obliquely signals the kind of "errors" he means to
correct and contain in the more rigorously purposeful story line
of his epic, while its speaker openly addresses the delay in the
military campaign undertaken by the soldiers of the cross.

Ah non sia alcun, per Dio, che sí graditi
doni in uso sí reo perda e diffonda!
A quei che sono alti princípi *orditi*[40]
di tutta l'opra il *filo* e 'l fin risponda.
                    (1.27.1–4, emphasis mine)

> Ah, before God, let there be none that would lose and dissipate
> such welcome gifts in such unworthy use! Let the weaving and
> completion of the whole work answer to those beginnings that
> are so loftily laid out.

Again, the promised end secures the whole in a purposeful
design and keeps at bay the danger of wasted opportunities, and
this mimesis of moral exhortation within the narrative echoes
the terms of literary theory that Tasso employs to elevate his

37

own intentions as a poet above the flaws in Ariosto's performance; for Tasso asserts that the wholeness of the *Furioso* depends upon taking the *Innamorato* into account, and such a massive work as their combination produces would violate Aristotelian precept by being more than an ordinary memory could retain after a single reading.[41] The ending of that "entire" poem would inevitably lose sight of its beginning, and vice versa; thus, the "errors" of plotting in Ariostan romance mirror the moral lapses that tempt irresolute crusaders whom Goffredo must rally to bring their mission to a conclusion.

Such graftings of literary theory upon poetic practice also take place in the speech of a pagan rival and thus suggest further undercurrents of poetic emulation in the ostensible conflict between Christians and Saracens. Alete's Odyssean eloquence summons terms from young Tasso's poetics as he attempts to persuade Goffredo to abandon his quest, the liberation of the Holy Sepulcher, and to make peace with the caliph and rest on his laurels. The king of Egypt becomes, in effect, the ideal reader of a dangerous romance whose power to enchant can disable Christian activism if this ambassador's rhetoric can transfer the experience that he aims to evoke onto his immediate audience:

> E la fama d'Egitto in ogni parte
> del tuo valor *chiare* novelle ha sparte.
>
> Né v'è fra tanti alcun che non le ascolte
> come egli suol le *meraviglie* estreme,
> ma dal mio re con *istupore* accolte
> sono non sol, ma con *diletto* insieme;
> e s'appaga in *narrarle* anco a le volte,
> amando in te ciò ch'altri invidia e teme.
> (2.62.7–63.6, emphasis mine)

And Fame has sown in every region of Egypt fresh tidings of your valor. Among so many there is not one who does not hear them as he is wont to hear the greatest marvels. But by my king they have been received not with astonishment alone, but with pleasure too; and he himself takes pleasure in recounting them at times, loving in you that which another envies or fears.

Although marvels, which especially abound in romance, are threatened by Tasso's drive to found his epic upon unimpeachable grounds, they are a sine qua non of heroic poetry that he refuses to abandon. Rather, he seeks to establish them on the secure basis of a divine machinery derived from "true religion," as we have seen in discussing Clorinda. Marvels elicit wonder, the definitive emotion of epic (according to Aristotle); for narration can convincingly represent actions that would appear ridiculous on stage. Further, marvels give pleasure, which Aristotle demonstrates by citing everybody's inclination to supplement stories with precisely this motive at heart.[42]

Young Tasso also refuses to abandon the ambition of producing pleasure through poetry. In addressing the readers of the *Rinaldo*, he seeks to reassure them about his neoclassical inclinations: "You will not find me bound to the most severe laws of Aristotle, which have rendered those poems less pleasant that otherwise would have been most pleasant to you. But I have only followed those precepts of his which will not take away your delight."[43] Further, in the early *Discorsi*, he claims that pleasure is the aim of the art that he practices; and he acknowledges that Ariosto, more than any other modern Italian poet, has achieved this goal.[44] Moreover, it is this ambition that ultimately gives rise to the most breathtaking stretch of prose that Tasso ever wrote, the oft-cited purple passage about the cosmic harmonies attained by reconciling the seemingly contradictory impulses of the one and the many. The poet, as divine artificer of the poem's universe, incorporates these rival pressures in discordant concord and thus accommodates their potential opposition in a larger whole.[45]

Ironically, two estimable critics, Benedetto Croce and Robert Durling, have anachronistically employed this magisterial image of the poet to characterize Tasso's seemingly inevitable archrival Ariosto, whose poetic persona, like his poetry, more often inspires contrast, than comparison, with Tasso's.[46] But this exalted ideal's applicability to its own advocate in many ways seems purely theoretical, for the Olympian mastery that Tasso envisions in his poet-god is often belied by the strain of emotional urgency felt in his poem. Even though his poetics strictly

39

curtails actual appearances of the poet *in propria persona*, highly charged currents of authorial feeling are often perceptible in the *Liberata*. The ideal of divine artistry in ultimate control comes to seem yet another flight from subjectivity whereby an appeal to traditional authorities, like this time-honored version of the poet-creator's *imitatio dei*, releases Tasso from personal accountability and the need to fashion a more immediate self to represent his own presence in his epic.

In the early *Discorsi*, where Tasso actually does give word to how a poet can speak directly in his own poem, he invokes the vatic ideal of prophetic transport. "When the poet speaks in his own person," Tasso writes, "he is allowed to think and speak as though with a different mind and a different tongue and much beyond ordinary usage because we believe him inspired and rapt with divine *furor*."[47] But this, too, is a role that Tasso per se shies away from, with the exception of brief outbursts like the apostrophe to Tancredi—though the poet does include, as an alter ego within the *Liberata*, Peter the Hermit, who provides him a venue for such sacred pronouncements. In his poem's initial invocation, however, Tasso introduces himself as a man caught between conventional extremes and somewhat at a loss for an unequivocal self-image. He wavers between being a conduit for heavenly inspiration and being a vulnerable pilgrim in need of refuge, both of which roles his redoubtable forerunner, Dante, manages to assume without paltering. Moreover, Tasso's prompt apologies for the potential duplicity of the craft that he practices highlight the ambivalence that he seems to feel in his dual identity at this juncture. Still, this exordium is the most sustained glimpse that we have of him throughout the poem—though even it concludes quickly.

Ariosto, on the other hand, often makes his voice clearly audible in the *Furioso*. For example, the proems that open each canto and the myriad shifts from one plot to another provide repeated occasions for the narrator's direct entrance into his ongoing story; and it is just these features of Ariostan romance that Tasso explicitly censures. He also condemns the indecorum of some of the *Furioso*'s more scabrous passages in a sequence of citations at the opening of the third of the early *Discorsi*, and these lapses in propriety clearly violate the canons of taste befitting the grand style that Tasso recommends for heroic poetry. But Aristotelian neoclassicism especially equips Tasso to disparage what appear as structural flaws from its perspective, which thus gives him an authoritative advantage over his daunting precursor; for multiplicity of plot is the conventional feature of medieval romance routinely sent up by Ariosto through willful interventions that exaggerate the arbitrariness of such shifts in narrative direction and also provide an opportunity for the poet's self-representation. Tasso, however, turns an apparently deaf ear to Ariostan parody in these maneuvers and finds them, instead, doubly vulnerable targets with even further qualities that invite negative critique.

Ariostan interruptions announce the fictionality of the poem-in-progress by dramatizing its dependent relation to the apparently arbitrary whims of its author, who, it seems, can intervene willy-nilly. Sometimes—Tasso notes in his preface to *Rinaldo*—Ariosto comes forward as a sort of reader's aide to clarify the complex ramifications of the many strands of plot that he is weaving together.[48] Sometimes, as his defender Giraldi avers in his behalf, he is skillfully orchestrating the action to increase suspense;[49] and Ariosto himself provides a version of this argument in his claim that he changes subjects to avoid boring the reader:

Ma lasciàn Bradamante, e non v'incresca
udir che cosí resti in quello incanto;
che quando sarà il tempo ch'ella n'esca,
la farò uscir, e Ruggiero altretanto.
Come raccende il gusto il mutar esca,
cosí mi par che la mia istoria, quanto
or qua or là piú varïata sia,
meno a chi l'udirà noiosa fia.

Di molte fila esser bisogna parme
a condur la gran tela ch'io lavoro.
E però non vi spiaccia d'ascoltarme,
come fuor de le stanze il popol Moro
davanti al re Agramante ha preso l'arme . . . [50]
(13.80–81.5)

41

But let us leave Bradamant: be not dismayed to hear that she remains imprisoned in the spell—when the time is ripe for her to be released from it, I shall bring her away, and Ruggiero too. As varying the dishes quickens the appetite, so it is with my story: the more varied it is, the less likely it is to bore my listeners To complete the great tapestry on which I am working I feel the need for a great variety of strands. Suffer me, then, to tell you about the Saracens assembling from their encampments to pass in review before King Agramant.

Although Ariosto protests that his desire to keep his readers entertained motivates such breaks in the flow of his narrative, frequently it is just when things are getting interesting that he turns his attention elsewhere. Sudden interruptions of this sort may seem to heighten suspense, as Giraldi claims—though the resumption of episodes thus brought up short often occurs at such a distance from the break that this effect has been entirely dissipated.[51] The "average memory" (to use Aristotle's phrase) simply could not be expected to recall what it last heard of the figures involved in the unfinished story. But whenever Ariosto makes such a peremptory move, the artificiality of his creation becomes unmistakably apparent, especially when he introduces a gloss in his own voice. He thus decisively marks the boundaries of the aesthetic space that his poem occupies by putting them emphatically on display.

Tasso's handling of transitions from scene to scene shows his concern to tighten the seams that stitch together his episodes and to "naturalize" the shifts from one incident to another. First of all, he holds the geographic center of his narrative with remarkable tenacity; for example, after the infernal council at the opening of canto 4, there is only one significant departure from the theater of war around Jerusalem until canto 13—Erminia's nocturnal outing and her pursuit by Tancredi, which occupy forty-seven octaves in a sequence of nine cantos otherwise situated entirely in the immediate vicinity of the city under siege.[52] In the midst of these excursions, Tasso manages the transition of narrative attention from Tancredi to Erminia, and vice versa, in a manner whose smoothness markedly differs from Ariosto's

42

treatment of such occasions. Tasso simply follows the thought processes of each character until he locates their absent object; and the move from the psyche of one to the circumstances of the other almost occurs in the mind of the former, thus predisposing the reader to make simple narrative connections without discontinuity. Two parallel phrases, *Intanto Erminia* (7.1.1) and *Tancredi intanto* (7.22.7), bracket an interval where both characters' simultaneous awareness of one another bridges whatever gap the passage from one place to another could open; and Tasso's total occlusion of his own part in arranging this transition further focuses the reader's attention on the poem's action, not on its manipulation at the poet's whim.

Tasso also subscribes to an ideal of the reading experience that makes *willing* suspension of disbelief seem merely a charade of credulity, for he means to make his poem irresistably engaging. Thus, he fully endorses the neoclassical value of *enargeia* in his early poetics: the poet "must not merely persuade [his readers] that the things he has written are true; he must also suggest them to their senses in such a way that they do not believe that they are reading but, rather, that they are present and they see and hear them."[53] Therefore, obvious violations of the spell cast by a story, such as Ariosto often allows, are inevitably anathema to Tasso. But one of the great thrills and surprises in reading the *Furioso* is how the mind can be reabsorbed in a story despite its obvious status as "mere" fiction and its undisguised subservience to such a capricious narrator's designs. Despite Ariosto's transparent stage managing of what seem simply marionettes, one can nonetheless find oneself actually caring about their fortunes and thus continually hovering on the brink of the supposedly "modern" realization that make-believe matters: imaginative experience counts enough to constitute a legitimate field of discourse in which feelings and values of "real" consequence are involved.

The sixteenth century is justly famous for its blindness to the modern distinction between fiction and falsehood,[54] and evolutionary accounts of the emergence of narrative genres regularly speak of the "rise" of the novel and the "aesthetic" as post-Renaissance phenomena.[55] However, modern romance's

43

indebtedness to Ariosto and Tasso should not be overlooked in historical reckonings that tend to see *Don Quixote* as a terminus a quo for the development of fiction as we understand that term today. Stephen Gilman's posthumously published study of Cervantes shows an especially keen appreciation of Ariosto's influence upon the "first" novelist; for he attributes to *Don Quixote* the collaborative awareness of the author as a fellow reader and not-so-secret sharer in the fictional experience that he offers to his audience. This mutuality of concern for self-evidently imaginary constructs at both ends of the reading process evolves from an appropriation of the self-conscious discontinuities in Ariostan romance that the current obsession with their "subversive" impact fails to grasp.[56] This kind of reading encourages participation in shared experiences of the imagination, rather than skepticism and alienation through the unmasking of their fictionality.

Of course, Tasso himself takes part in such a failure to distinguish between fiction and lying because his urgent concern with authoritative truth values as secure grounds for epic narration apparently makes him insensitive to Ariosto's parodic artistry or, at least, unappreciative of its exploitable possibilities. (Indeed, for him there are none in this regard.) Yet Tasso's poetics also constitutes a significant step along the way in the progress toward modern fiction because he explicitly addresses the issues raised by this Ariostan legacy that Cervantes so triumphantly inherits. If we must employ an historical model and thus subscribe to something of a "Whig idea" of the emergence of novelistic fiction, Tasso deserves a place in that account. For example, his preoccupation with poetic license (*licenza di fingere*) in the early *Discorsi* indicates his exploration of kindred concerns, as do the Canon of Toledo's borrowings from his theories in *Don Quixote*.[57] Furthermore, even when Tasso cites one of Ariosto's most blatant debunkings of the veracity of a traditionally accepted authority, he makes a slight concession that suggests his recognition of Ariosto's intentions in this regard. For when he quotes Saint John's lunar revelation of the "truth" about the Trojan war,

che i greci rotti, e che Troia vittrice,
e che Penelopea fu meretrice
(35.27.7–8)

that Greece was vanquished, Troy triumphant, and Penelope a
whore,

he allows that this "falsehood" suits Ariosto's purpose in its
context. Thus, he reveals a capacity to appreciate Ariostan
irony, however remote it may be from his own temperament and
ambitions.

The high seriousness of Tasso's aesthetics puts an extreme
value upon the earnest response that heroic poetry aims to elicit
from its audience. Therefore, Ariostan intrusions upon the spell
of narration that his poem, on occasion, powerfully casts violate
the ultimate effects deemed appropriate for epic. Even at moments of the most poignant pathos, Ariosto impishly makes his
presence felt and thus qualifies the full impact of the emotions
that such narrative events can summon. For example, in a poem
that relentlessly exposes the self-centeredness of erotic passion
there are, nonetheless, two pairs of memorably selfless lovers:
Zerbino and Isabella, Brandimarte and Fiordiligi. However, Ariosto arranges the death scenes of one member of each of these
pairs in such a way as slightly to compromise their grave claims
upon us just when they have reached their loftiest pitch of exalted feelings. Rather than yielding to the superior force and
sexual demands of Rodomonte, Isabella practices a ruse upon
him that brings about her own decapitation while thus preserv-
ing her pure devotion to her dead lover. The scene dramatizes an
ethereal fidelity that accepts death, rather than surrendering to
hostile circumstance, even under great duress. Yet Ariosto mis-
chievously attends to the material details of Isabella's immediate
postmortem moments by counting the bounces when her head
hits the ground; and he thus effects a spasm of descent in the
tone, as well as in the part of the body in question:

Quel uom bestial le prestò fede, e scórse
sí con la mano e sí col ferro crudo,

che del bel capo, già d'Amore albergo,
fe' tronco rimanere il petto e il tergo.

Quel fe' tre balzi; e funne udita chiara
voce, ch'uscendo nominò Zerbino,
per cui seguire ella trovò sí rara
via di fuggir di man del Saracino.
                    (29.25.5–30.4)

The brute believed her and used his hand and his cruel sword to
such effect that he lopped her fair head, once the abode of love,
clean from her shoulders.
    Her head bounced thrice: from it a voice could be clearly
heard pronouncing the name of Zerbin, to follow whom she had
found so novel a way to escape from the Saracen.

Similarly, when Brandimarte breathes his last after being
slain in the decisive battle at Lipadusa, the experience of exceptional loss is poignant in the fullest sense of the word. This death
moves the poet directly to address "our Father in heaven" and
to call the fallen hero nothing less than a martyr. But after a
brief intermission—first for the canto's end and then for that of
the battle—we return to the moribund Brandimarte and hear
his final words. This inevitably dramatic speech concludes with
a botched attempt to name his beloved, but his affecting last
gasp gains a compromising prominence by its terminal place-
ment as a rhyme word. Three out of the five syllables in
Fiordiligi's name thus neatly fit the formal pattern, though the
rest is silence until the poet supplies what is missing. However,
the artificiality of the poetic structure notably obtrudes because
of this incomplete utterance; and the rhyme's suddenly more
noticeable presence awkwardly qualifies the purity of the moment's emotion.

Orlando l'elmo gli levò dal viso,
e ritrovò che 'l capo sino al naso
fra l'uno e l'altro ciglio era diviso;
ma pur gli è tanto spirto anco rimaso,
che de' suoi falli al Re del paradiso
può dimandar perdono anzi l'occaso;

46

e confortare il conte, che le gote
sparge di pianto, a pazïenzia puote;

e dirgli:—Orlando, fa che ti raccordi
di me ne l'orazion tue grate a Dio;
né men ti raccomando la mia Fiordi . . . —
ma dir non poté:— . . . ligi—, e qui finio.
E voci e suoni d'angeli concordi
tosto in aria s'udîr, che l'alma uscío;
la qual disciolta dal corporeo velo
fra dolce melodia salí nel cielo.

(42.13–14)

Orlando drew the helmet off his head to find his brow cleft down
to the nose. Even so, Brandimart had enough life in him yet to
ask pardon for his sins from the King of Paradise before his day
waned, and to encourage the count, whose cheeks were bathed
in tears, to bear up.
        "Orlando," he asked, "remember me in your prayers to God.
No less do I recommend you to my Fiordi . . ." but before he
could say "ligi" he was finished. And the music and harmonious
voices of angels could be heard in the air, for his spirit, freed of
its bodily vesture, took flight to heaven amid sweet melody.

This open revelation of poetic design does not by any means
decisively undo the quality of feeling already generated by this
event. Rather, as I have already suggested, it promotes a consciousness of fictionality that stops short of subversion and invites
the mutual participation of author and reader in a reckoning with
their serious share in this merely make-believe moment. However, Ariosto's uncourtly failure to disguise his artistic strategies
and its affinity with the un-Aristotelian self-consciousness that
Tasso deplored in the *Furioso* must remain in the foreground of
our attention because they are central to the young poet's response to his most challenging predecessor.
        An awareness of these sour notes or disenchanting effects as
typically Ariostan, even at moments when the most elevated
emotions are at stake, makes the response of Leone's inter-
locutors to his story of Ruggiero's ultimate chivalry all the
more worth exploring. When Leone elaborates the long chain

47

of improbable heroics, amatory stratagems, and marital ambitions that link his life with Ruggiero's and (almost) with
Ruggiero's wife-to-be, Bradamante, the theme that holds his
story together is the absolute heroism and self-sacrifice of its
recently converted protagonist. Chivalric idealism in its loftiest
register would be hard put to imagine a more worthy exemplar
than Ruggiero during the immediate past, and Leone's tale of
this paragon touches the hearts of all of its auditors:

> E con sí dolci affetti il tutto espresse
> che quivi occhio non fu ch'asciutto stesse.
> (46.63.7–8)
>
> He told his tale with such sweetness that there was not a dry eye
> in the audience.

To rephrase Ariosto's original so that it corresponds to a plati-
tude of theater criticism, "there was not a dry eye in the house."
When we recall the primary authority of Aristotle's treatise on
tragic drama in Tasso's early theorizing about epic, such a histri-
onic model hardly seems ill suited to construe this romance
episode's impact upon those who hear it told within the tale
itself.

Leone's apparent success in this narrative transaction may
derive from the approaching conclusion of the poem itself. At
this juncture, the poet may have felt constrained both to wrap
things up more tidily than has been his wont heretofore and to
recuperate the ostensible values of his chivalric romance in a
final gesture of affirmation despite previous demonstrations of
their fallibility. Then again, Leone's success may only be apparent; for stable perspectives and referential certainty uncompromised by doubt and irony do not exclusively obtain even as the
Furioso draws to a close.[58] Still, judging this storyteller's success
by criteria that derive from the Stagirite's aesthetics bespeaks
the crisis in narrative art that occasioned the midcentury debates about heroic poetry; and it also points to the conveniently
limited amount of theory that Aristotle actually wrote about
epic. Unlike the missing treatise on comedy, which left a potentially daunting void for aspiring philosophers of that genre, the

brief remarks about narrative in the *Poetics* invited elaboration while supplying an authoritative point of departure. Epigones had to feel neither overwhelmed by precedents so extensive as to defy assimilation and adjustment nor entirely without premises from which to extrapolate. The mid cinquecento's need for a vernacular classic in narrative poetry that would share the status of Petrarch's lyrics and Boccaccio's *novelle* in their respective genres was nicely complemented by a theoretical lacuna in Aristotle's text that was waiting to be filled.[59]

But the pressures that Tasso felt in undertaking to compose a modern epic were not entirely literary; nor was the dangerous unorthodoxy of Ariosto's art several decades after that poet's death exclusively a matter of aesthetics. Tasso faced age-old dilemmas of earnest religious artistry in an atmosphere of heightened sensitivity to matters of doctrine and church government. Saint Paul had memorably subordinated eloquence to charity; and Jerome had suffered an oneiric cudgling at the hands of an angel who accused him of affecting Ciceronianism, rather than simply demonstrating pious devotion.[60] However, the sixteenth-century experience of Erasmus (whose mock encomium of Christian folly and philological study of biblical translation closely affiliate him with Saint Paul and Jerome, respectively) bears more directly upon Tasso's efforts to inherit Ariosto's legacy in the tradition that he sought to advance. For the madness of Orlando and the overall thematization of insanity in the *Furioso* have a potentially Erasmian dimension that critics have long acknowledged;[61] and the cure of Orlando's mania brings the poet into his most open engagement with the authority of Scripture, which figures so decisively in the religious debates of the sixteenth century.[62] But what Tasso was likely to make of Astolfo's lunar encounter with Saint John the Evangelist half a century after its initial publication differs radically from the sort of response Ariosto may have legitimately expected in 1516, just prior to Luther's first famous salvo against Rome; and the experience of Erasmus with Martin Dorp as his reader provides an illuminating perspective upon this distinction between the two poets.

In his epistolary response to Dorp's objections to the *Moriae*

49

encomium, Erasmus records the sort of explanations necessary when irony is inaudible and traditional authority is threatened. Among the major points of Erasmus's self-defense is a rhetorical clarification of the "ethos" of his speaker, Folly, that in terms of narrative theory, would equate with considerations of point of view. In reading the *Moriae encomium*, such understanding becomes relevant from the opening attribution, *Stultitia loquitur* ("Folly speaks"); for if we consider the source of everything that follows, we should be protected against taking it too seriously— even though Erasmus claims, in the prefatory letter to Thomas More, to have "praised folly in a way not wholly foolish."[63] Such rhetorical niceties, however, elude earnest auditors like Dorp, or else they are simply irrelevant to their primary concerns; and Erasmian levity comes to seem a grave challenge to the ecclesiastical and political establishment. Another key element in the letter to Dorp deals with problems of biblical translation and the authority of Jerome's Vulgate. In this regard, Erasmus speaks as the foremost humanist of his era; and his philological expertise serves as a basis for pursuing questions about the authorized version of Holy Writ that so disturb his correspondent. If you are familiar with the historical cliché that Erasmus laid the egg that Luther hatched, you may here scent the unmistakable odor of the henhouse. While the "canonization" of *Orlando furioso* was the work of Ariosto's midcentury proponents, the "de-canonization" of certain biblical texts took place at the hands of northern reformers who took Erasmus' lead farther than he himself was willing to go.[64]

Tasso, of course, lived in a period later known to Protestants as the Counter-Reformation, when the Church of Rome's resistance to such interrogations of scriptural authority was well under way. In 1559, for example, the Council of Trent was in its fourteenth year and thus almost contemporary with, the laureate-to-be of Ferrara, when it officially placed all of Erasmus' books on the *Index librorum prohibitorum* and thereby branded them as unsuitable reading for the faithful.[65] Other edicts of that body attempted to shore up the shaken foundations of the Vulgate's authority by proclaiming it authentic and its translator inspired; thus, the church of Rome aimed to transcend historical philology's merely rational deductions with dogma and revelation.[66] Tasso himself steered clear of the Bible as a source of narrative material because of the sacred doctrines that were founded upon it and the consequent lack of freedom for invention that would hamper the poet who tried to adapt stories from that holy text. Tasso's circumspection in this regard betokens inhibitions unknown to Ariosto and provides a ground for comparison between the two that helps us to understand the final stage in young Tasso's narrative theory, as he was bringing the *Liberata* to a conclusion in 1575–76. For, at that stage in the writing of his poem, Tasso composed an allegory for his epic, supplying this overall interpretive key to replace his neo-Aristotelian poetics as a prefatory guide to the *Liberata*.

Tasso came to write an allegory for his epic somewhat reluctantly. His misgivings about doing so have led to the accurate perception that he felt compelled to protect his poem from censorship by providing a high-minded rationale for its vulnerable passages; but that insight about his motives by no means implies that the allegory is merely a postfactum addition without any organic connection to the *Liberata*. Recent critics have convincingly demonstrated otherwise.[67] In the process, however, they tempt us to find secure meanings in the very aspects of Tasso's poem that disclose instability and danger symptomatic of his cultural moment and indicative of his own second thoughts as he composed his epic.[68] The desire for a snug fit between the allegory and the poem or between the history of Tasso's ideas that demonstrate how he developed the allegory and the resultant document itself may lead us to overlook the space between them and the tensions that these gaps betray. Comparison with Ariosto and the Erasmian elements in the *Furioso* can help us reopen issues that too secure a sense of the allegory's applicability foreclose prior to investigation.

Tasso overcomes the Aristotelian injunction of rigorous self-effacement on the narrator's part by a kind of ventriloquism that we have already witnessed vis-à-vis his neoclassical principles. For example, when we are privy to a God's-eye view of the assembled crusaders in the first canto, we may fairly sense the narrator's own drive for stuctural unity in the plot of his poem, especially when we recall Tasso's deployment of the traditional image of the poet as divine artificer in the early *Discorsi*:

> Gli occhi in giú volse, e in un sol punto e in una;
> vista mirò ciò ch'in sé il mondo aduna.
>
> (1.7.7–8)
>
> [The eternal Father] turned his eyes below and saw in one moment and in one glance whatever the world contains within itself.

Allegory entails a pressure toward unity in terms of theme that parallels the Aristotelian urge for unity of plot; thus, it is understandable that critics sense in young Tasso's great paean to the creation's variety-in-unity a pivotal moment where the overall coherence of allegorical meaning seems to impend, although the explicit subject under discussion in that passage is narrative structure. In fact, Tasso's "Allegoria del poema" rewrites or extends the earlier poetics in another area, as well; for Tasso forewent the discussion of poetry's civic function at the opening of *Discorsi dell'arte poetica*, and his main concern with the reader's response subsequently focused upon Aristotle's specification of wonder as the characteristic emotion of epic.[69] The poet becomes a dutiful citizen in his "Allegoria" when he stresses moral edification as his poem's central ambition.

Tasso's allegory encodes an ethical message in the *Liberata* that various figures like Peter the Hermit and Ugone di Vermondois decipher at crucial moments in the plot (1.31, 14.13). Tasso thus inscribes the gist of his explanatory preface within the text of his poem, and such internal glosses from a third party manage to disable the neo-Aristotelian critique of the poet's speaking in his own voice that Tasso previously endorsed. This sort of inside expositor is also a feature of the *Moriae encomium* and *Orlando furioso*—though in both of these cases, the readers-within-the-text provide interpretations of a more unsettling kind. In a shocking exposé of their lack of referential value, Erasmus' Stultitia expounds the signs of office traditionally worn by princes and prelates and various other functionaries of church and state.[70] She asserts that these symbolic claims of authority are belied by conduct that completely fails to measure up to the signals sent by such ceremonial paraphernalia. Many of Erasmus' readers inevitably responded in sympathy with these resonant denunciations of the temporal and spiritual hierarchies of the early sixteenth century; but such reactions, like Martin Dorp's, were beyond Erasmus' control. The impulse-to-reform within the pages of Folly's oration struck a responsive chord in the larger world of political and religious activism. Just as Luther would attempt to draw the line at the Peasants' Revolt, Erasmus would try to discredit Luther's extreme developments of his own tendencies toward personal piety and scriptural sanctions. However, regardless of the original intentions of such authors, these matters had developed a momentum of their own; they were out of the hands of whoever may have given them a start.

Similarly, Ariosto seems to "subvert" almost every major premise upon which Tasso meant to found a stable poetics of epic (history, religion, and allegory, for example) if we read the *Furioso* with the sober earnestness of post-Tridentine Italy and ignore the redemptive tradition of Pauline folly that may transform the apparent nihilism of such "subversions" into a liberating break from what often passes for wisdom in the world. For example, Ariosto's regular citations of Turpin to authorize patent absurdities makes a mockery of the romance appeal to traditional *istorie*, which is precisely Ariosto's ambition in thus sending up this convention of twice-told tales premised upon familiar, accepted sources; but Tasso's goal of founding epic upon historical records also suffers a potential diminishment in this light, especially when the epoch that he particularly favors for heroic poetry turns out to be the age of Arthur and Charlemagne.[71] Invocations of Turpin's authority, offered as conclusive evidence of the veracity of the most bizarre improbabilities, occur throughout the *Furioso*. They are one of the poet's comic routines. When Orlando rescues Zerbino from the henchmen of Count Anselmo d'Altariva, he wreaks extravagant havoc upon them; and Turpin provides the body count with typical mock precision:

> Di cento venti (che Turpin sottrasse
> il conto), ottanta ne periro almeno.
> (23.62.1–2)

53

Out of one hundred and twenty, at least eighty perished (these are Turpin's figures).

When the mad Orlando runs amok, we are told that Turpin provides the record of the particularly far-fetched "miracle" of a lucky survivor's escape (29.56.5–8); and when Ruggiero jousts against Mandricardo, the same witness is enlisted to attest that the splinters of their lances ascended to the sphere of fire, whence they returned aflame (30.49.1–4).

Other such instances abound, and they all shamelessly exploit this wonderful comic resource. However, Ariosto's parody of this romance convention can also raise ironic suspicions about Tasso's desire for the credibility of historical records upon which to found his narrative. This aim earnestly motivates his quest for material suitable for epic poetry, yet such doubts set these two poets once again at apparently cross purposes. William of Tyre's account of the First Crusade is hardly exacting in its obedience to the rules of evidence; indeed, to expect such rigor from a twelfth-century chronicle is thoroughly anachronistic. The medieval archbishop's record of events is unsurprisingly interspersed with providential claims and biases. Further, the liberty that it left Tasso to employ his own powers of invention constituted a good part of its appeal to him. Still, this avowed poetic license reveals the emphatically rhetorical function of the truth claims made by Tasso for such sources; and their potential emptiness of referential value could haunt his poem with the specter of Ariostan skepticism.

Likewise, when Charlemagne cuts a deal in prayer with God in canto 14 of the *Furioso*, the subsequent descent of Michael from heaven deploys allegorical figuration in irreverent jest. If construed with the gravity typical of Counter-Reformation piety, such a parodic intercession from above fully compromises the method practiced by Tasso in the *Liberata* to represent the throne of God, whence the same divine messenger is dispatched to constrain the demonic disruption orchestrated by the infernal powers (9.56–57). Although Charlemagne's appeal is laden with orthodox formulas of devotion, he ultimately sounds like a pitchman who persuades God to go along with his wishes because

God will look bad if God's avowed enemies win the battle against his ostensible adherents. Further, the divine intervention occasioned by Charlemagne employs such allegorical agents as Discord and Fraud, thus achieving its ends via mediators usually identified with heaven's adversaries, rather than with the forces of good. Tasso's allegorical entities on high (Space, Time, and Motion, to name only three) contain none of these vexing associations. They fit their place in the poem, whereas the abstract executors of God's will in the *Furioso* are disturbingly incongruous if they are taken too seriously. As Tasso knew, some of his readers were likely to do so; Silvio Antoniano demonstrated this fact with annoying regularity.

Astolfo's lunar outing with Saint John the Evangelist condenses this "deconstructive" potential of Ariostan romance vis-à-vis Tasso's aesthetics in a memorable episode during which the author of the Fourth Gospel functions like Peter the Hermit in Tasso's poem or Stultitia in Erasmus' mock encomium: he reads the moon's landscape as a symbolic stand-in for earthly affairs in a manner that fully discloses the arbitrariness and absurdity of the claims for allegorical correspondence made by the saintly interpreter.[72] Further, he offers a theory of literature that both undermines utterly any pretense that poetry may have of historical veracity and, coincidentally, undoes in a devastating addendum the authority of Scripture, as well (35.23–28). That we take him at his word in these matters is a paradox worth acknowledging or an opinion worth disputing: if all writers are liars, trusting the admission of this shortcoming by any particular one of their number entails an exception to the very rule that he is enunciating. Although Tasso shows an inclination to appreciate some of the irony at work in this passage, his sensibility in general bespeaks a moment more likely scandalized than amused by such high jinks. During the Counter-Reformation, a Dorpian inaptitude for the vertiginous intensities of *serio-ludere in extremis* reached something like epidemic proportions—a phenomenon that the fortunes of Erasmus' writings emphatically demonstrate. The official proscription of his complete works as reading matter unacceptable for members of the Roman Church is symptomatic of the spirit of the times. Ariosto, of course, continued to be widely read; but his prestige was not unassailable. Rather, it occasioned widespread debate, especially once the alternative of Tasso's epic emerged as a rival position from which to mount an attack.

Allegory, for Tasso, thus functions as a guarantor of acceptable intentions in the face of potential censorship like that suffered by Erasmus,[73] rather than as a sure guide in the right direction for a comprehensive interpretation of his poem, regardless of how Tasso's preface may present itself. This limit on that introductory document's utility does not occur merely because all readings are partial and provisional. Certainly, the inevitable bias of any critical response warrants frank acknowledgement; and allegorical readings of the *Liberata* do tend to concentrate on canto 13 and convenient clues scattered more sparingly elsewhere in the text. But a preoccupation with this sort of symbolic coherence in Tasso's narrative also occludes the poet's formative reckoning with the new classicism that pervaded his milieu and served, especially, to put Ariosto's otherwise daunting renown in a perspective more manageable for a youthful aspirant to his popular esteem. Tasso opens "Allegoria" with an assertion of poetry's double nature that gives mimesis equal partnership with allegory in the art that he is about to propound from the alternative angle of the latter mode. Readers of the *Liberata* need to give ample attention to the neo-Aristotelian aspect of Tasso's aesthetics, even though it is openly relegated to secondary status on this occasion; for that school of poetics had priority during most of the time that Tasso spent fashioning his masterwork. His later statement gained the prominence of a preface for reasons of self-defense in a literary environment of notable austerity. The "Allegoria" is by no means a mere smoke screen, but its interpretive value needs to be viewed in the context of Tasso's era and his changing sense of the *Liberata*'s chances in the world into which he was about to release it.

Romancing the Word:
Neo-Aristotelian and
Protestant Poetics in
Tasso and Spenser

The development of a distinctively Protestant poetics derived in good part from the central position of the vernacular Bible in the Reformation.[1] Lay reading and interpretation of Scripture without the traditional mediation of church authority helped to constitute a new relation between the biblical text and its Protestant readers; and the invention of printing facilitated the widespread dissemination of that sacred volume in language accessible to a much broader readership. Thus, the biblical text began to be wrested free from received opinion and increasingly opened up to a new range of responses. The novelty of such changes occasioned alarm that bears witness to a vertiginous sense of the possibilities unleashed by the altered circumstances of Bible reading in the Reformation. For example, Jack Wilton, the hero of *The Unfortunate Traveller* by Thomas Nashe, expresses a strong desire to reform the reformers themselves who have taken such dangerous liberties with Holy Writ and thereby created treacherous illusions that tempt the faithful with errors of doctrine. Written in the 1590s, Nashe's fictional account of the Munster Rebellion of 1534 features this outburst of exasperation against the Anabaptists from Jack, a supposed eyewitness of the event:

> In the days of Nero there was an odd fellow that had found out an exquisite way to make glass as hammerproof [i.e., hammerable] as gold. Shall I say that the like experiment he made upon glass, we have practised upon the Gospel? Ay, confidently will I. We have found out a sleight to hammer it to any heresy whatsoever.

> But those furnaces of falsehood and hammerheads of heresy must
> be dissolved and broken as his was, or else I fear me the glittering
> glass of innovation will be better esteemed than the ancient gold of
> the Gospel.[2]

Humanist philology, impelled by evangelism, did much to
give rise to the situation that Jack Wilton here deplores; and the
distinctively Protestant quality in early modern poetics owes its
origins to such scholarship conducted, often enough, by literati
with no great appetite for church reform once such movements
had gained an irresistible momentum. Among scholars, Erasmus felt himself obliged to deplore the extremes quickly reached
by certain positions that he had initially endorsed; and among
narrative poets of the first rank in early modern literature, there
is a pattern of development that charts a comparable course.
The humanist recovery of classical models for imitation required
a negotiation with Christian orthodoxy and innovation that can
help us discriminate among the achievements of Tasso, Spenser,
and Milton; and their respective relations to the biblical text and
to the canons of ancient literature provide especially telling perspectives for such an endeavor.

For instance, Tasso explores the topic of appropriate subject
matter for heroic verse in the first section of his early poetics;
and his endorsement of the exemplary legacy of Homer and
Virgil promptly raises questions of religion. According to Tasso,
the divine machinery of classical epic, which employs the Greek
pantheon, as well as its Roman reincarnation, is ill suited for a
Christian poet, as the unfortunate example of Trissino's *Italia
liberata da'i goti* makes plain. Pagan gods have no place in a
modern epic, though the marvels accomplished by divine intervention are too important to the success of such narratives to
sacrifice them altogether. Therefore, the angels and demons of
Christian tradition can serve in their stead and effect similarly
wondrous turns of plot without violating a contemporary audience's standards of credibility. The tenets of modern belief remain unchallenged in this rationale for an orthodox otherworld.
In fact, their secure hold upon the minds of Tasso's anticipated
audience serves as an essential premise in his argument. How-

ever, when Tasso entertains the notion of stories from Scripture as suitable subjects for heroic poetry in his time, he rules such material out because of the doctrines founded upon it. Retelling such tales amounts to dangerous tampering with sacred lore and with faith itself. Certain stories have certain meanings attached to them in their received form; and because those meanings are precious, it is best to leave such stories alone.

The hazards of retelling function here like those of interpretation in Jack Wilton's disparagement of innovative expositors of the Gospel. Heresy lurks both in unlicensed readings and in artful reprises of sacred texts. However, Tasso's alarm at uncontrolled narration finds its most noteworthy expression in terms of neo-Aristotelian poetics and a preoccupation with literary form, rather than in the exegetical novelties of Bible-reading agitators for changes in church government. Ariostan romance with its cornucopian proliferation of plots occasioned in Tasso the dizzying angst that unrestrained interpretation of Scripture promoted in English poets who aimed to inherit the mantle of their Italian precursor.[3] Both Spenser and Milton understood the kinship between the central issue of genre theory that Tasso faced in trying to come to grips with *Orlando furioso* and the crisis in religious authority occasioned by the Protestant rallying cry of *Sola scriptura*. Both of them also tried to put that insight to work in their own epic endeavors.

Because Aristotle prescribed unity as a prime desideratum in the plots of narrative and dramatic poems, Tasso felt that he had, in evaluating the achievement of Ariosto, unquestionable authority to cite. This classical precept decisively exposed the essential shortcoming of Ariostan romance and guided Tasso in his own efforts to discipline the unruliness of form that characterized *Orlando furioso* and constituted his chief complaint against it. Since he was unabashedly eager to attain popular success like that of his main precursor, he wanted to preserve the appealing qualities of Ariosto's poem (its amours and enchantments, for example); but he aimed to contain the digressions that gave rise to such episodes within a unified story line capable of accommodating temporary deviations without complete loss of direction. When Tasso was bringing the *Liberata* to

59

a conclusion, unities of an order other than the structural began to preoccupy him increasingly; and he elaborated a thematic argument that explained the allegorical coherence of his poem. In this scheme, principles of form are fully moralized; and the "errors" of romance become imbued with ethical culpability to an extent previously unrealized in the neo-Aristotelian aesthetics of Tasso's early *Discorsi*. This shift in emphasis highlights an interesting correspondence with Spenser's allegory in the opening canto of *The Faerie Queene* that as far as I can tell, has been overlooked heretofore.

In Tasso's "Allegoria del poema," the corporate unity of the Christian army stands for the moral equilibrium of the human person attained through right government of the passions under the rule of reason. The impulsive errantry of wayward knights ultimately yields to the appropriate discipline of a single commander in chief and thus enables the Crusade to achieve its original purpose. Beneath this ethical gloss subsists a structural principle whereby epic contains the centrifugal tendencies of medieval romance, and the moralizing of such hybrid songs (to adapt Spenser's phrase) seems almost inevitable; for the clean separation of thematic and structural features is often a convenience for argument's sake in literary theorizing, rather than evidence that these elements exist in a pure condition in the practice of poetry. But we can observe an evolution in Tasso's attitude toward his own poem that shifts the weight given to these somewhat artificial categories. As we move from the neo-Aristotelianism of his early *Discorsi* to the Platonic morality of his "Allegoria," thematic concerns prevail over matters of form. But this very fluidity in the terms that characterize the qualities of the genres in question leaves them open to appropriation for a range of purposes. Tasso's altered perspective on his own poem in the course of its composition merely exemplifies a process that the *Liberata* also undergoes further from home (if you will), at the hands of other writers.

Spenser's debt to Tasso is discernible at certain obvious points in *The Faerie Queene*. The Bower of Bliss, for instance, comes easily to mind, as does the reference to Tasso's "Rinaldo" and his "Godfredo" as exemplary poems for the "poet historicall" in the letter to Sir Walter Ralegh from the 1590 edition of books 1–3.[4] Spenser would have known Tasso's "Allegoria," since it was regularly published in editions of the *Liberata* after first appearing in 1581; and *Discorsi dell'arte poetica*, which Tasso once meant to print as a foreword to his epic, had first appeared in print in 1587, though they were written as much as a quarter of a century earlier. Spenser's commitment to "overgo" Ariosto had been made public in a letter from Gabriel Harvey that appeared in 1580;[5] and book 3 is so saturated with Ariostan echoes that Spenser's emulous ambitions with regard to the *Furioso* are still undeniably motivating him.[6]

Spenser intended his poem to be an allegory from the outset; and the very sort of accusations sometimes leveled at Tasso to discredit his claims about the *Liberata*'s full participation in that mode inspire Spenser's explanation of his "continued Allegory or darke conceit" in the letter to Ralegh. Skeptics argue that Tasso devised his allegory to avoid censorship by putting a uniformly edifying construction upon his poem and thereby pre-empting those powerful critics who could deprive him of the privilege necessary for publishing it. Such doubts can be confirmed, at least in part, by Tasso's correspondence, which he had no intention of making public before the *Liberata* appeared in print.[7] Spenser, on the other hand, promptly acknowledges his dual desire both to avoid "gealous opinions and misconstruction" and to explain the overall purpose of *The Faerie Queene* in his epistle. Unlike Tasso, he openly admits his apprehensions about the hostile environment into which he is releasing his work; and he aims as much to avoid misappropriation as to promote right understanding. Tasso, of course, was no stranger to either ambition; but he does not own up to the defensive impulse that in part occasions the allegorical reading that he supplies for his poem.

Because of Tasso's profound commitment to mimetic realism *all'Aristotile*, even the most patently symbolic events in his narrative are embedded in circumstantial details of the ongoing action. They may acquire their own explanatory gloss to heighten their allegorical import—as occurs, for example, in Peter the Hermit's exhortation when Goffredo is being proposed as the sole supreme commander of the Crusade at the poem's start and in Ugone of Vermondois's appearance to him in a dream vision to encourage the recall of the erring Rinaldo (1.31, 14.13). Yet such incidents refer to a credible sequence of recognizably earthbound events and constitute part of a transcendent experience fully integrated into the narrative's historical sequence. Thus, Peter the Hermit's argument for Goffredo's exclusive claim to command seems a natural representation of his expression of an opinion entirely relevant to both the moment and the matter at hand at this stage of the story; yet his immediate political position advocating the choice of Goffredo alone as captain of the army precisely echoes the allegory of reason's rule over the passions and further suggests the structural disciplining of errant episodes in the unified plot; and Ugone's oneiric intervention suggests a similar range of references while remaining within the operative conventions of realistic representation governing Tasso's poem. The poet's extravagant later assertion of the identity of history and allegory in *Gerusalemme conquistata* actually seems fulfilled in this speech of Peter's in the first version of the epic; for the entire gamut of Tasso's dominant preoccupations—from Aristotelian unity of plot in subject matter drawn from history to allegorical signification—momentarily converges at this juncture.[8] He is in fact, however, adjusting the chronicler's record handed down to him by William of Tyre. That account tells of no such unanimity among the chief figures of the Crusade in their choice of an overall leader. Rather, Tasso's formal commitment to unity of plot and his thematic claim to allegorical coherence determine his version of the events, which he relates in accord with the canons of neo-Aristotelian realism.

An event similarly laden with kindred concerns promptly occurs in the opening canto of *The Faerie Queene*. Examining it from a comparative perspective with Tasso in mind can help us to distinguish both the continuities with the neo-Aristotelian poetics of genre theory and the differences characteristic of the Protestant environment in which Spenser produced his poem. The choice of Holiness to occupy first place in the sequence of virtues addressed by his poem indicates the priority of the religious question in Spenser's England: it demanded immediate

62

attention even if the pleasures of Ariostan pursuits with their innumerable enchanting detours may have originally appealed more to the poet's own inclinations. The allegorical import of Spenser's poem is well advertised. Not only the letter to Ralegh but the interpretive epigraphs prefixed to each canto and plentiful signs in the course of each episode make this abundantly clear. On the other hand, Spenser's occasional descents into the details of mimesis are anything but sustained; thus, his echoes of Tasso's neo-Aristotelian poetics are more surprising and harder to discern because they are inevitably entangled in other kinds of representation. At first, the Redcrosse knight's initial combat against Errour in the service of Una may only resonate slightly with an awareness of the terms of Tasso's reading of Ariostan romance; but recognizing that connection can lead to a deeper appreciation of the various influences working upon Spenser at this point in his poem.

The terms themselves may seem obvious indices of Spenser's preoccupations; but their transparency also causes problems, because of the many constructions to which it easily permits them to yield. The poet himself wisely refrains from giving Una a name until the forty-fifth stanza of canto 1, thus allowing her to accumulate significance through action before fixing her with a label. In fact, he only makes that definitive gesture at the very moment when the deceptive possibility that there may be more than one of her has become fully realized by Archimago's creation of an illusion in her form to trick Redcrosse. But the reader's awareness that the poem is thoroughly imbued with allegory predisposes him to respond in abstract terms with alacrity; thus, the late announcement of Una's name hardly occasions a shift of perspective, as would an entirely new vista opening before him. Errour, on the other hand, is promptly identified in an edifying discourse by Una as soon as Redcrosse and his wards enter the vicinity of his den (1.1.13). This dragonlady is a known enemy from the outset, but her particular qualities unfold in the encounter that follows this forewarning.

The errors of romance worried Tasso due to their ability to distract a poet from the purposeful completion of a single story

63

and to entangle him in myriad alternative tales whose number ultimately knew no necessary bounds. Since that genre apparently could breed narratives ad infinitum, its potential for doing so needed to be contained by an overriding principle of unity that could keep chaos at bay by its superior claims. Aristotle authorized such a principle for Tasso, who enlisted that authority in absolute terms to make his case in the early *Discorsi*; and his poetic practice likewise disciplined the impulsive divagations of knight-errantry within the resolutely purposeful design of an epic project—the delivery of Jerusalem from pagan control. Ultimately, for Protestant poets, there was only one story; and certainly, there was only a single text that told that tale with final authority. Even if the Bible included many narratives, skillful exegetes could typologically assimilate them to the terms of a master plot that told all. Early Christians had thereby adapted the Hebrew scriptures to their new dispensation and thus saved those texts for their enlarged canon. Ideally, for Protestants, the Bible could serve to stabilize the centrifugal impulses occasioned by the desire for reform; and the Word of God in the Book could provide a secure ground upon which to stand and challenge the *consensus fidelium* claimed by the Roman church.[9]

But the world into which Spenser released the first half of his magnum opus by no means corresponded comfortably to these ideals of Protestantism. Rather, a babel of controversy and constant apprehensions of schism characterize the context appropriate for a reading of the 1590 *Faerie Queene*; and the initial episode of that poem culminates in a nightmarish image symptomatic of the Reformation in one of its traditionally definitive features. When Errour vomits a gush of texts, she seems a grisly revelation of the darkest "consequences of [one of those] inventions" singled out by Francis Bacon as having "changed the state and appearance of the whole world."[10] Errour, in her death throes, discloses an unsettling affinity with one of the enabling technologies of the new epoch, the printing press. Edward Halle's oft-cited account of the bishop of London's futile efforts to contain the circulation of Tyndale's New Testament details a previous failure in a mission ironically akin to that of the Redcrosse knight in his first encounter. Cuthbert Tunstall's buying of books for the purpose of burning them merely provided Tyndale with revenue for subsequent editions of the offending volume. In the eyes of this ecclesiatical opponent of innovation a new monster indeed was at large in the land.[11]

Calling Errour's textual vomit a "nightmare" bespeaks the realm of dreams when the imagination at rest can fall prey to its most intimate demons, not the "slomber of delight" induced by "that sweet verse, with *Nectar* sprinckeled, / In which a gracious seruant pictured / His *Cynthia*, his heavens fairest light." (3.proem.4.4–9) In other words this episode allows a haunting presence to emerge even in the process of recounting its demise, and shades of this monster return in various forms hereafter. The threat of demonic recidivism remains in some minds even beyond the apocalyptic finale of Book 1. Among "the raskall many . . . / Heaped together in rude rablement" who gawk at the triumphant champion,

> One that would wiser seeme, then all the rest,
> Warnd him not touch, for yet perhaps remayned
> Some lingring life within his hollow brest,
> Or in his wombe might lurke some hidden nest
> Of many Dragonets, his fruitfull seed.
>
> (1.12.9–10)

Likewise, Spenser employs an Ovidian simile of spontaneous solar generation in the mudflats along the banks of the Nile to depict the writhing contents of Errour's foul regurgitation (1.1.21); and then he returns to exactly this figure in a strikingly different context (3.6.8.7–9), the birth of Belphoebe and prelude to his description of "[s]o faire a place, as Nature can devize" (3.6.29.3): the Garden of Adonis.

The dreamlike infusion that we call a "nightmare" is not the divine afflatus bestowed upon the vatic poet at the behest of a heavenly muse; rather, it lurks in the margins of consciousness to ambush the unsuspecting, who can be misled by (among other things) zeal and overconfidence. While the apocalyptic resonance of Redcrosse's initial encounter only becomes fully audible during his climactic duel in Edenland, tokens of such significance appear in the opening episode. For example, Errour's "filthy parbrake" recalls "the three uncleane spirits like frogs" witnessed by John of Patmos in his vision as they "come out of the mouth of that dragon, and out of the mouth of that beast, and out of the mouth of that false prophet"; and early Protestant expositors of this passage seem secure in the knowledge of its import. In the Geneva Bible of 1560, Revelation 16.13 carries this marginal gloss: "That is a strong number of this great devil the Popes ambassadours which are ever crying and crocking like frogs and come out of the Antichrists mouth, because they should speake nothing but lies and use all manere of craftie deceit to maintaine their rich Euphrates against the true Christians."[12]

Such confident apprehension of the enemy by no means obtained throughout the nation whose queen Spenser celebrated in his "poem historicall." The sort of frustration experienced by the bishop of London in his attempts to stem the flow into England of Tyndale's New Testament takes on different forms once that book circulates legally and reaches readers previously more inclined to leave its interpretation to others. For example, in a sermon delivered at Saint Paul's Cross in 1589, Richard Bancroft complains of text-torturing Protestant expositors. Although he clearly opposes what a later age would come to call the magisterium of the Catholic Church (that is, its teaching function, especially in regard to biblical interpretation), Bancroft is also alarmed by unqualified readers of Holy Writ who put strains upon passages from that sacred text and wrest meanings from them that lead to heresy and schism. Thus, Bancroft cites Augustine to the effect that "faithful ignorance is better than rash knowledge" and goes on to invoke Gregory of Nazianzus' assertion, "It falleth not within the compas of everie mans understanding to determine and judge in matters of religion: *Sed exercitatorum*: but of those that are well experienced and exercised in them."[13]

Bancroft's distress at the liberties taken by inexperienced readers participates in the mounting anxiety over Protestant tendencies that seem to be spinning out of control in the Elizabethan 90s. In "Satire 3" Donne addresses a command to his readers that sounds exactly like the quest that Redcrosse has undertaken. Donne enjoins them to "seek true religion"; but immediately, a question follows: "O where?" Then the poet proceeds to catalogue the throng of rival claims that vie for priority and threaten to distract believers from the unique goal worthy of their sustained efforts. Thomas Nashe's version of the Munster Rebellion in *The Unfortunate Traveller* specifically relates this problem of theological error to freedom of scriptural interpretation. Given his career as a picaresque trickster, Jack Wilton, the hero of Nashe's perversely polymorphous creation, seems an odd sort to decry revolutionary religion in the guise of a defender of the faith. His credibility here ranks with that of Falstaff when he denounces Prince Hal's "damnable iteration" of a passage from Proverbs.[14] If we recall Nashe's conservative participation in the Marprelate controversy, this righteous voice of angry reaction can be traced to a likelier source. But even Jack betrays a sense of the personal incongruity of such pietistic ranting when he describes himself as "duncified betwixt divinity and poetry"[15] in the process of making the transition from this episode to the next in his story.

In this moment of self-consciousness as a narrator, Jack expresses a feeling of generic indecorum when he finds himself straddling the boundary between prose fiction and homiletics; and his puzzlement over discursive propriety points to a formal issue with thematic consequences that is very much alive in the opening of *The Faerie Queene*, where Spenser's preoccupation with theological error corresponds to the structural feature of romance that particularly concerned Tasso. The dizzying proliferation of plot lines in *Orlando furioso* first moved Tasso to enlist the authority of Aristotle to condemn his precursor's seemingly random habits of narration. Subsequently, Tasso employed allegory to thematize, prominently, this potential for chaos in the genre that he sought to incorporate and transcend in his epic. Spenser was certainly acquainted with this symbolic transformation in Tasso's prefatory "Allegoria del poema," where the haunted wood outside Jerusalem becomes a Platonic figure for the "errors of opinion." Cutting down this forest enables the epic action to proceed to its conclusion in a manner far more decisive than any closure that Ariosto brings to bear upon his rambling tale. Just as Redcrosse slays Errour while in the service of Una, Rinaldo's triumph over the enchantments of the forest saves Tasso's poem from the errors of romance and thereby guarantees its unity of plot—a structural accomplishment in terms of neo-Aristotelian poetics that acquires explicit allegorical significance in the preface to the *Liberata*.

A wood of this sort appears at the outset in *The Faerie Queene*, where Spenser represents it via an epic catalogue and thus effects a generic merger of notable originality in what could seem simply a conspicuous reprise of Chaucer. Similar signals of genre and mode abound in this passage, and their shrewd deployment displays a subtlety of poetic craft that was more fully theorized by Spenser's Italian coevals than his Tudor compatriots; for Spenser's inheritance of both his classical and modern precursors sometimes seems retarded by the belated emergence of humanism and literary theory in northern Europe, and the old joke about England's being the ideal place to be when the world ends because everything there happens at least fifty years late seems a fit comment at numerous junctures in *The Faerie Queene*. However, familiar assertions of Spenser's lack of historical discernment, like those made by Thomas Greene and Frank Kermode,[16] warrant interrogation and skepticism when we review the opening of his poem.

For example, much has lately been made of Spenser's fashioning for himself a literary career in the image of Virgil, as the beginning of the proem to book 1 clearly demonstrates.[17] However, historical philology had not yet decisively demonstrated the spurious (that is, un-Virgilian) origins of the *Aeneid*'s traditional incipit when Spenser rendered those very lines into English at the outset of *The Faerie Queene*. From this perspective, he got off to a pretty bad start for someone who wanted to sound like the Augustan laureate! But Spenser ends up making the very gesture that such philologists deem to be their own insight, for he begins book 1 proper with his own *arma virumque*: "A Gentle Knight was pricking on the plaine, / Y cladd in mightie armes and silver shielde." Thereby, he laid claim to what a subsequent age might complacently call the "authentic" Virgil resurrected afresh by the discriminations of historical scholarship.[18]

68

Imitating the Italians of whatever vintage tests both a poet's reading comprehension and his historical consciousness. But historicism of the latest variety is likely to slight, or overlook, the former, especially when such critics establish their position via a polemic with formalism. Stephen Greenblatt's discussion of the Bower of Bliss omits even the mention of its source in Tasso, while positing romance as the genre of desire, which is then discussed in terms of Freudian psychoanalysis.[19] Jeffrey Knapp's analysis of the Errour episode focuses on two literary kinds, pastoral and epic, while neglecting romance, the very genre that the monster's name encodes.[20] Of course, these fine critics are attending to other priorities; but their ambition to account for the cultural pressures absorbed and refracted in Spenser's text need not suppress the literary history that impinges upon it, as well.

The assimilation of romance's distinctive divagations of plot to ethical errors was a conventional way of moralizing such songs long before the Reformation; but preoccupations with heresy and the vagaries of "freelance" exegesis become especially acute as Protestantism gains ground via print technology, which multiplies such concerns exponentially. Errour is a sort of apocalyptic bookmobile previously unimaginable yet compounded of elements of a familiar literary legacy. She betrays Spenser's anxiety on the brink of a decade of profound religious uncertainty and contestation whose more radical impulses he had formerly defended in their earlier manifestations. But the champion of Grindal in the age of Whitgift begins to experience more feelingly the differences between idealist and *politique* trends in progressive Protestantism, though such emotions may only emerge indirectly in an episode which seems decisively to eliminate such threats.[21] On the surface, Redcrosse, the designated agent of righteousness, appears to put an end to such dangers once and for all through his ultimately successful action against Errour.

Spenser read Italian narrative poetry through the lens (or prism?) of its early modern reception insofar as that process had made itself felt in his remote angle of the world. Harington's Englishing of the *Furioso* represents the results of more than a half-century of defensive responses to Ariosto's beloved, but increasingly problematic, romance. In setting it forth in 1591, the Tudor poet followed continental precedents and filled its margins with helpful glosses that should have comforted the reader who desired a modern "classic." They point out its frequent references to ancient worthies like Virgil and Ovid; note "invocations," "similes," "sentences," and other such features marking the highest style and sentiments; and guide the reader from the abrupt interruption of an episode to its resumption elsewhere, lest he should feel frustrated or confused by Ariosto's apparently random picking up and dropping of story lines.[22]

The opening of *The Faerie Queene* reveals the incorporation of such classicizing ambitions into the body of the poem itself. Conspicuous allusions promptly lay claim to a Virgilian pedigree for Spenser's poem, and the muse gets her call in good time. Lengthy similes serve as hallmarks of the loftiest genre, and the sensible sound of proverbial wisdom is audible in Una's counsel or in such a dramatically conclusive hexameter as "God helpe the man so wrapt in *Errours* endlesse traine" (1.1.18.9). While the poem features its own modest apparatus in the explanatory subtitles to each book and the recurrent quatrains at the head of each canto summarizing the action-to-come, the gist of the most typical marginalia in Harington has been silently absorbed into the poem itself. Spenser has smoothed over transitions and eschews the sometimes violent interruptions that Ariosto willfully perpetrates and for which Harington, like previous publishers on the continent, felt a need to compensate with notices of the story's continuation further ahead. Moreover, Spenser never indulges in the coy teasing that often accompanies such Ariostan routines.

The rigor of Tasso's Aristotelian scruples rendered these sudden shifts less tolerable to him, and the multiplicity of plots thus occasioned aroused a premonitory anxiety in Tasso reminiscent of the nightmarish gush of texts in Errour's last gasp. Imagining a distracted poet faced with an unstoppable proliferation of plot lines, Tasso betrays a striking befuddlement in the face of Ariostan habits of composition.[23] Hard-line Aristotelianism,

70

with its insistence upon unity of plot, offered a safe haven from the daunting possibility of such disorder; and initially, it secured Tasso in his opposition to Ariosto's willful appearance of random narration. Platonic allegory subsequently supplied further assurance when Tasso was bringing the *Liberata* to a close in the mid-1570s, and he thus transformed its structural unity into thematic unity via the abstract coherence of sustained symbolic moralization.

Spenser likewise enlists that ancient tradition to provide an orderly rationale for a threatening profusion of substance in the Garden of Adonis. Chaos subsists as the ground of all being in the heart of that "joyous Paradize"; and awareness of this unique source for the multiple forms that come into existence should reassure us of their essential unity despite appearances to the contrary. However, in that sunny locale of benign fecundity, the central presence of Chaos, "[in] hatefull darkness and in deepe horrore" (6.36.7), may belie the consoling claims made in behalf of such a conventionally daunting vortex. Where Whirl is king, we may shudder despite all assertions that everything is under control. Chaos, like the Grim Reaper (of whom we hear shortly thereafter, 39.3), unforgettably qualifies such claims of orderliness and formal decorum and irrepressibly haunts this otherwise amenable locale. Furthermore, the grim counterpart of this Edenic site may indeed be the dragon, whose last gasp is never quite finally over and done.

Spenser's most thoroughgoing imitation of Tasso occurs at the end of book 2. The episode of the Bower of Bliss, while obviously owing something to Homer's *Odyssey*, amounts to a sustained reprise of Rinaldo's amorous malingering in Armida's palace from cantos 15 and 16 of *Gerusalemme liberata*. This section of *The Faerie Queene* includes numerous passages that are best described simply as translations of Tasso's Italian, though some decisively Spenserian inflections are audible at crucial junctures. The poetry here is erotically charged, and critics have been inclined to give Tasso credit for that. Further, they see in some of Spenser's addenda an anxious impulse ultimately to

71

censure and contain the indulgence of sexual feeling that his sources allow him boldly to portray further than he could have managed entirely on his own.[24] Recent criticism has incorporated political perspectives in its response to this passage; and the repressive violence of Guyon's destruction of this all-too-amenable locale has been assimilated to the iconoclasm of early Protestant reformers, the use of force by Elizabethan overlords in Ireland, and the conduct of European adventurers toward native populations in the New World.[25] Apologists for Spenser's severity, like C. S. Lewis, have recommended reading this episode in tandem with that of the Garden of Adonis to recuperate the damage done by the extremism of Guyon's supposedly exemplary behavior chez Acrasia.[26] The pairing of these two passages aims to illustrate Spenser's healthful affirmation of the positive force of human sexuality when it is rightly directed toward procreation in marriage.

Although the themes of these discussions—sex and politics—undeniably deserve their due, a comparative approach to *The Faerie Queene* can bring questions of poetics tellingly to the fore because it inevitably leads us back to Spenser's major sixteenth-century precursors, Ariosto and Tasso. Since critics in the cinquecento used literary theory to analyze the masterpieces of these two poets and since Tasso himself was a theorist of great distinction, issues from the debates over classical epic and modern romance necessarily pertain to Spenser's heroic undertaking in those genres; for the legacy he thus sought to inherit was saturated with such concerns despite their belated arrival in England, where rhetoric prevailed over poetics in most works of literary theory during the sixteenth century. The Bower of Bliss is a natural port of entry for comparatists due to its obvious derivation from the *Liberata*; but its conventional companion piece, the Garden of Adonis, which amounts to an ample discourse on human creativity, directly addresses matters of form and substance entirely relevant to the terms of neo-Aristotelian poetics in which controversies over *Orlando furioso* and *Gerusalemme liberata* were routinely conducted. Finding these topics at stake in contexts that have customarily occasioned other sorts of responses opens fresh vistas upon familiar grounds in Spenser's poem. In fact, comparative reading of such passages in *The Faerie Queene* can bring into view a line of development that clearly links Ariosto, Tasso, Spenser, and Milton through a series of formal and thematic concerns and a series of imitative reprises of recognizable pre-texts. For example, the congruence between the Spenserian context of heretical literary production and Tasso's horror at unbridled narration is by no means coincidental. Rather, it betokens the realization and development of potentialilties latent in the terms that this English poet inherited from his Italian forebears and thus transmitted to his own heir, John Milton.

This view of the Errour episode enables us to read it in relation to the Garden of Adonis with Tasso in mind; for the apparently desirable fecundity of that fertile retreat, which critics traditionally contrast with the sterile vampirism in Acrasia's bower, seems like the bright side of the uncontrolled production of narratives that Tasso dreaded. In the garden, form contains the proliferation of substance without inhibiting it; and the primal injunction of the divine word—"to increase and multiply"—is harmoniously fulfilled without overwhelming excesses. The "endlesse progenie" brought forth under these auspices behave themselves "according to their kindes," exemplifying the generic propriety whose lack Tasso lamented in Ariosto; and the "old Genius" who presides at the gates of this garden stands in distinct contrast to his evil double whom Guyon handles so roughly at the entrance to the Bower of Bliss. Conscientious recycling helps to maintain the balance in this ecosystem; for after a millennial interlude of restorative vegetating, "fleshly corruption" and the costs of being in the world are overcome, and once-naked babes can be again "clad with other hew" and returned to the earthly realm of mortality for a fresh start.

But there is another, more primal source of things within the precincts of the Garden of Adonis; and Spenser's brief mention of this gloomy place of origin notably shadows the sunny benevolence of constant procreation in this otherwise pleasant site.

> For in the wide wombe of the world there lyes,
> In hatefull darknesse and in deepe horrore,

73

An huge eternall *Chaos*, which supplyes
The substances of natures fruitfull progenyes.
(3.6.36.6–90)

The grim abode of this ever-dependable provider opens like an abyss in paradise; and broaching this topic here, however slightly, offers a chilling reminder of "the griesly shade" whence all things emerge. Although this acknowledgment leads to a further discussion of the ravages of time, brevity is a noteworthy feature of this hasty reckoning with an ominous aspect of incessant fecundity; and such concision serves to keep chaos emphatically at bay. Spenser's celebratory mood only yields momentarily to premonitions of disorder before promptly resuming its affirmative tone and insisting upon the eternal durability of substance despite the perishable forms that it temporarily takes. But, as always, such insistence may indelibly reveal the threatening demon that it intends to exorcise; and chaos unforgettably haunts this paean to continual creativity and the forms that accommodate its products.

Milton's portrayal of the fallen Lucifer in the opening books of *Paradise Lost* clearly and skillfully employs the resources of this legacy from his Italian and English precursors. When Satan volunteers, with impressive bravado, for the solitary mission of investigating and undoing God's new creation and creature, his solo adventure is characteristic of heroic undertakings in chivalric romance, especially as Tasso responded to their digressive movement away from the corporate center typical of epic discourse. Milton signals as much with the language in which he chooses to describe "this uncouth errand sole" and "wand'ring quest." The centrifugal energy of knight-errantry finds its embodiment here in demonic vainglory exposed with varying degrees of subtlety and directness as the episode proceeds. Allegory is the mode of choice when Spenserian echoes begin to abound during the parodic family reunion with Sin and Death, whose names themselves are indices of Milton's excursion into sustained abstract figuration. Although an overlay of Homeric elements from the *Odyssey*'s description of Scylla compounds the literary lineage of Satan's firstborn, the portrait of Sin is obviously indebted to that of Errour in the opening canto of *The Faerie Queene*. Her monstrous brood of cannibalistic offspring and "her bestial train" are recognizable borrowings from Spenser's dragonlady, as is her dual nature, which, beginning in the womanly, trails off into the serpentine.

Milton also makes a connection like the latent one in Spenser's poem between Errour in Redcrosse's initial combat and the glimpse of Chaos in the Garden of Adonis. The aptness of this juxtaposition becomes apparent in Tasso's early *Discorsi*; for it is the potential chaos in the errantry of Ariostan romance that causes the young poet to shudder so memorably while he argues passionately on behalf of Aristotelian unity of plot as a means of avoiding such unsettling disorder.[27] Appreciating the appropriateness of pairing these two episodes also preempts some of the attention customarily paid to the association of the Garden of Adonis with the Bower of Bliss; for the peril entailed in "Errours endlesse traine" precisely suggests what amounts to one of the scariest aspects not only of Chaos but of the garden's ostensibly benign fertility—its *endlessness* and the loss of formal control that nonstop proliferation portends. That Sin should thus get out of hand constitutes an essential tenet of Milton's theological perspective upon postlapsarian humanity; and we see this development in embryo as Satan's daughter allows him to pass through Hell's gate. On his way to the world, his "wand'ring" course takes him through a place

> where eldest Night
> And Chaos, ancestors of Nature, hold
> Eternal anarchy and by confusion stand,
> . . . .
> The womb of Nature and perhaps her grave . . .
> (2.894–97, 911)[28]

Milton's final formulation in these lines suggests the complete subversion of a source initially celebrated by Spenser for its unceasing fecundity: a womb has become a grave, perhaps. But that possibility inheres in the Spenserian pre-text of which Milton frequently shows a consciousness in this part of *Paradise*

Lost; and a comparative awareness of both the theoretical premises and the poetic practices that these English writers are drawing upon in these instances can significantly illuminate this surprising evolution in the epic tradition from Ariosto to the Restoration.

Milton's
Change of Note:
Italian Precedents
for Tragedy in Eden

Milton's debts to Tasso as both a poet and a theorist are manifold, and the English poet explicitly acknowledges them on several memorable occasions.[1] However, by openly incorporating theory into *Paradise Lost*, Milton manages to merge the two roles more thoroughly than Tasso deems proper; for in the proem to book 9, Milton engages in a sustained excursion on the principles of poetics operating at that juncture in his poem. He thus indulges, on this occasion, in such an extended discourse in his own voice as a poet as Tasso, invoking Aristotelian precept, pointedly censures Ariosto for routinely addressing to his readers in the proems of *Orlando furioso*.[2] Barbara Lewalski sees Horace's "Epistula ad Pisones" as the generic model for the passage in *Paradise Lost*; and this verse letter's traditional name, the *Ars poetica*, clearly indicates the theoretical nature of Milton's authorial interpolation.[3] To find a comparable exposition of poetics by Tasso, we need to turn to his prose writings, especially *Discorsi dell'arte poetica* from the 1560s, which contain his theories most relevant to *Gerusalemme liberata*.

In these early *Discorsi* Tasso quibbles with Aristotle about the differences between epic and tragedy in order to specify a further distinction between the two genres. Thus, he is engaged in exploring concerns very much akin to those that preoccupy Milton in the proem to book 9. In his prose discourse, Tasso questions Aristotle's equation of epic action with its tragic counterpart and consequent expression of the identity between heroes from each type of work. Tasso argues that since each kind of work produces its own distinct effects, these divergent results must arise from different causes. In other words, tragedy produces pity and fear in the beholder, whereas epic promotes wonder; thus, these diverse emotions must arise from distinguishably various sources. Both sorts of hero may be illustrious, but they do not embody the same kind of illustriousness. More generally accessible kinds of characters can stir our compassion because our ordinary humanity readily relates to theirs; but only high types (whose actions, it is crucial to note, may embody extremes of *either* virtue *or* vice) can occasion our wonder, the definitive response elicited by epic.[4]

In the proem to book 9 Milton acknowledges his poem's mixing of the genres that Tasso takes pains to distinguish even further than his ancient mentor. On the brink of reporting catastrophe in Paradise, Milton specifies the change of note about to take place in his poem; and the terrible transformation that subsequently occurs produces the effect that both Aristotle and Tasso would predict. After the Fall, Adam and Eve are no longer out of human reach in their pristine innocence and primal dignity. They are more like us than we may enjoy acknowledging—reproachful, acrimonious, despairing, and prone to repeating, ad infinitum, the new-found errors of their ways. We can all too readily relate to behavior like theirs.

Due to their fall into ordinariness, our original progenitors are no longer so dauntingly above average and thus recall the Italian precedent that Tasso was most eager to exclude from the tradition he inherited; for by a surprisingly kindred turn in his plot, Ariosto degraded the wise Roman senator who serves as the eponymous hero of his chivalric poem. The etiology of Orlando's madness derives in good part from the everydayness of the disappointment that he suffers. Having risked all against knight-errantry's finest exemplars in the contest for the princess of Cathay, Orlando goes round the bend when he learns that Angelica has fallen for a foot soldier. The debasement of this preeminent paladin's erotic loss to a "vilissimo barbaro," a "povero fante," (42.39, 42.45), functions as a powerful provocation of Orlando's *furor*. The heroic cavalier cannot abide the indignity of such comeuppance and loses his grip entirely, with the same lavish extremism that characterizes his martial exploits in the Christian cause.

By calling the offending infantryman Medoro, Ariosto explicitly signals his representative mediocrity. Medoro stands for the *aurea mediocritas* (golden mean) that epic heroism, in Tasso's view, must eschew. Ariostan irony, however, inscribes a subtler, less diametrical contrast between Orlando and his rival than the famous paladin's high-mindedness allows him to perceive; for Medoro is demonstrably a hero. Angelica succumbs to his charms while ministering to the wounds that he incurred in a bold effort to rescue his fallen leader from the enemy; but physical courage is not what singles Medoro out to her, and it is irrelevant to what drives Orlando mad on his account. Angelica's disregard crazes Orlando, and her preference for a virtual nonentity from the rank-and-file powerfully compounds the offense that he takes at seeing undeniable evidence of her rejection.

Milton's theoretical interlude also bespeaks another uncanny congruence between the poetics of *Paradise Lost* and Tasso's reading of *Orlando furioso*; for the occasion upon which Milton announces his change of note amounts to his most sustained intervention *in propria persona*, interrupting the action of his poem to address his audience directly. Of the four proems, that to book 9, with its metanarrative reflections, is the only one not cast in the form of a prayer. Even if the other exordia tend to run to greater length than their classical models, this mode assimilates them to the conventional invocation of the muse in epic poetry and thus sanctions their presence, to a degree, in terms of neoclassical values. The proem to book 9 shifts to a different register of discourse to announce the imminent tragedy and to rationalize its presence in "heroic song."

In his preface to *Rinaldo*, Tasso summoned Aristotelian norms to censure Ariosto about authorial interventions in the *Furioso*; and he also applied the courtly cinquecento term *affettazione* to elaborate his neoclassical objection to Ariosto's lack of self-restraint in his own voice as a narrative poet.[5] Milton is uninhibited by the sort of rigor with which Tasso brought such strictures to bear upon himself and his chief precursor. Rather,

Milton's personal voice recurs freely throughout his poem and glosses the action in a manner structurally similar to Ariosto's editorial obiter dicta.

Of course, Milton's tone differs notably from the ironic detachment typical of the *Furioso*'s author. Even when he appropriates Arisoto's most extravagant claim for the innovative boldness of his project, Milton's prophetic daring in summoning inspiration for his "advent'rous song" contrasts starkly with Ariosto's relaxed, low-key references to "quel furor che suole"— the usual fury of poetic transport—that he claims he must transcend to feel equal to the obligatory task of eulogizing his Este patrons (3.1.5).[6] Ariosto's breezy offhandedness in such dealings with what he actually calls prophetic illumination ("quel profetico lume ch m'inspiri," 3.2.6) is anything but Miltonic. However, the opportunity for direct discourse in the process of telling his story is a liberty that Tasso rules out on the basis of Ariosto's practice, while Milton allows himself this freedom and employs it most fully in justifying the tragic nature of his poem's penultimate agon. The seriousness with which Tasso views such first-person interventions by the poet himself becomes clearer when we note the exception that he made for prophetic speech of the very kind characteristic of Milton's sustained passages in his own voice.[7] Tasso's own unwillingness to grant himself this permission within his own poem, even though he has justified it in theory, bespeaks the unique severity of his self-restraint in this regard. Thus, the prophetic poet of the *Liberata*, whom critics like Joseph Wittreich fashion as an obvious precursor to the vatic Milton, is decidedly inchoate in Tasso's actual self-representations in his masterwork.[8]

In many ways, it was Ariosto's indecorous style that particularly scandalized Tasso's sense of the magnificence proper to epic diction; and the nonchalant colloquialism with which his popular precursor represents the appeal for inspiration epitomizes this defective feature of the *Furioso*. The third of the early *Discorsi* addresses elocution, the last of the three rhetorical categories that organize that treatise; and Tasso therein assembles a series of Ariostan gaffes (willful, no doubt) to exemplify the impropriety that he means to censure in the *Furioso*.[9]

Consisting mostly of scabrous passages, these selections strike tones that Milton's grand style never sounds, so that no area of agreement exists here between Milton and the precursor who exacted the most thorough reckoning from Tasso. Rather, it is the introduction of tragedy into *Paradise Lost* that brings these unexpected parallels between Ariosto and Milton to light; for the accessible humanity of heroism that the tragic genre entails and the authorial intrusion into the narrative that Milton employs to clarify the exigencies of the tragic turn in his plot both demonstrate curious affinities between Milton and an Italian poet whose characteristic temperament, in general, diverges notably from that of the English Puritan's overall high seriousness.

According to Milton, Tasso is the only modern poet whose work offers an exemplary model of the "epic form"; and his theories of this art, Milton feels, teach "what the laws are of a true epic poem."[10] Such endorsements make an investigation into the role of tragedy in *Gerusalemme liberata* even more germane in an attempt to reckon with both Milton's Italian forerunners and the crucial significance of that genre in *Paradise Lost*; for although Tasso distinguishes tragic protagonists decisively from the epic variety and although he theoretically rules them out of heroic poetry, not only do figures of this sort appear in the *Liberata*, but Tasso also marks them as such, indicating thereby his conscious deployment of one generic code in the service of the larger designs of another. This compositional strategy approximates the method that Milton makes explicit in the proem to book 9; but the mixture of genres also threatens to undermine Tasso's overall ambitions in ways that Milton manages to control more effectively.

When Tancredi realizes the tragic mistake he has made in slaying none other than his beloved Clorinda, Tasso labels his recognition with an obviously Aristotelian tag: "Ahi conoscenza!" Further, to stress the generic signals that he thus sends, he leads into this exclamation with repeated variations on the conspicuous term's verbal root as well as those of a kindred word. But the correction of Tancredi's painful error is promptly undertaken with the baptism of his dying beloved, and both Peter the Hermit's homiletics and a vision of Clorinda in heaven occur with alacrity to keep the Christian paladin from slipping permanently into the wrong kind of plot.

Likewise, when Rinaldo hears of Goffredo's intention to punish him like an ordinary soldier for killing Gernando in a duel in defense of his honor, he ominously interprets the motives of the commander in chief as a desire to mount a tragic spectacle for the enemy:

> Fera tragedia vuol che s'appresenti
> per lor diporto a le nemiche genti.
> (5.43.7–8)

> It is a bloody tragedy he means to present to the enemy troops for their pleasure.

But this indignant aristocrat then takes his leave to wander in the appropriate way for such a hero: the errors of romance claim his energies for much of what remains of the poem. The patent literariness of the language Tasso employs in both of these instances is an indirect means for communicating messages akin to what Milton explicitly addresses to his readers in the proem to book 9.

But the pagan heroes ultimately seem consigned to the genre that Tasso meant to exclude from this kind of poem. Argante suffers death in what seems a theatrical space after giving voice to his ruminations upon the fated fall of Judea, the kingdom he has striven to uphold. When he and Tancredi, who are implicit rivals for the unattainable Clorinda, finally face each other in single and solitary combat, Tasso offers the word *teatro* as a likely label for the site chosen for this encounter (19.8.7). Furthermore, he has previously "staged" another such duel in similarly dramatic terms. When Tancredi pursues Erminia under the illusion that he follows his beloved Clorinda, he arrives at Armida's magic castle, where the renegade Rambaldo challenges him to single combat. Tasso sets that scene with a simile that clearly signals his conscious staging of this encounter like a dramatic spectacle:

> Splende il castel come in teatro adorno
> suol fra notturne pompe altera scena.
> (7.36.5–6)

82

The castle glows as does the lofty stage in a decorated theater
amid festivities at night.

But Argante's meditative speech presses this congruence of context further by its open expressions of tragic sentiment. Before
engaging in his duel to the death with Tancredi, he first pauses
to contemplate the city, visible in the distance, and fully to savor
its fated fall despite any efforts of his own:

"Penso," risponde, "a la città del regno
di Giudea antichissima regina,
che vinta or cade, e indarno esser sostegno
io procurai de la fatal ruina."
                              (19.10.1–4)

"I am thinking," he answers, "of the city, most ancient queen of
Judah's realm, that now she is falling in defeat, and vainly I
undertook to be a prop against her fatal ruin."

Likewise, Solimano pauses in the midst of the final fray and
beholds an all-inclusive vision of the tragic destiny of our condition. He, too, becomes a pensive witness to the final battle in
terms pregnant with signs of the rejected genre:

Mirò, quasi in teatro od agone,
l'aspra tragedia de lo stato umano:
i vari assalti e 'l fero orror di morte,
i gran giochi del caso e de la sorte.
                              (20.73.5–8)

He watched, as if in a theater or a stadium, the bitter tragedy of
the human condition, the various assaults and the fierce horror
of death, and the mighty casts of fate and fortune.

The pathos here is high, perhaps *in extremis,* if we are inclined
to press in the direction of the sort of heroism that Tasso
deemed appropriate for epic. However, its effect is remarkably
congruent with Aristotelian precept, as well; for it invites emotional participation so compellingly that the poet himself,
shortly hereafter, narrates the death of Solimano from *inside*

83

that figure. Two stanzas (20.105–6) sustain a simile that evokes in ample terms the interior condition of the beleaguered sultan. Then the poet completely drops the mediating terms of comparison and simply recounts the coup de grace as it appears to the victim:

> Giunse all'irresoluto il vincitore,;
> ed in arrivando (*o che gli pare*) avanza
> e di velocitade e di furore
> e di grandezza ogni mortal sembianza.
> (20.107.1–4, emphasis mine)

The victor comes up to the irresolute, and in arriving surpasses (*or so it seems to him*) all human semblance in swiftness, and in fury, and in greatness.

Such temporary fusions of the poet's perspective with that of a hero are by no means unprecedented in classical epic; but since this episode explicitly employs the language of tragedy and produces that genre's effects upon the poet himself, the purity of its kind seems hardly to meet Tasso's standards.

Fortunately, Tasso's poem often transcends his theoretical prescriptions, and a pedantic rigor in bringing them to bear upon the *Liberata* might indicate that a reader has fallen prey to the worst tendencies of the post-Tridentine legalism in both faith and poetics that haunted its author. Tasso's brave efforts directly to confront the crises of authority that characterize the religious and literary discourses of his age guaranteed that he would share in some of their shortcomings. A significant measure of his high achievement lies in his refusal to dodge central issues of his historical moment despite the painful consequences that they inevitably entailed.

Because his poetics explicitly deny him access to biblical stories as subject matter for heroic song, Tasso lacked Milton's opportunity authoritatively to bring about what we may fairly call a reversal of misfortunes—not only tragedy with a happy ending, as in Aeschylus' *Oresteia* or Sophocles' *Oedipus at Colonus*, but Christian tragedy with a vision of eternal salvation for humankind.[11] Adam's felix culpa occasions a fortunate fall (as even he himself seems to divine), whereas the crusaders' *glorioso acquisto* sponsors the bloody triumphalism of temporary military supremacy. Such Christian heroism, unqualified by ordinary humanity, entails an off-putting austerity; thus, the pathos of the losers in such an endeavor can even make their narrator waver in his allegiance to the side of the angels in his poem. Milton's reliance upon Holy Writ as a ground for epic narration enables him to make claims that remain out of reach for his chief Italian precursor, yet they are filtered through a figure who has become utterly accessible in his postlapsarian condition of all-too-human fallibilty. Michael shows and tells Adam a story that he frequently misapprehends, and these errors serve as a measure of the tragic lapse from blissful innocence that he has undergone. But even through his fallen eyes traces appear of a brighter vision than any that Tasso could represent with the stability and conviction of his prime English inheritor.

Milton's vatic presence pervades his poem via Ariostan structures that Tasso censured, but Milton eschews the tone of ironic everydayness that Ariosto routinely employs to deflate grandiose pretensions in the traditional material that he reproduces.[12] Furthermore, the differences between Tasso and Milton in the matter of self-representation pertain both to a central issue of Tasso's poetics and a constant cause of debate among Milton critics; for the reception of Milton's poem entails the legacy of neoclassicism that ultimately derives in good part from Tasso's aesthetics. John Dryden and Joseph Addison, for example, objected to what they deemed Milton's entirely willful mixture of conventions from the two distinct genres of epic and tragedy.[13] More famously, neoclassical rigor led Doctor Johnson to deem all four of Milton's self-consciously bardic invocations "extrinsic" elements that compromised the integrity of his plot, though the incidental pleasures they provide made him refrain from wishing for their removal from the text.[14]

With the dawning of romanticism, Milton's stage-managerial intrusions were potentially less of an aesthetic problem; but the forces that they sometimes sought to contain became vulnerable to heterodox reconstruction. Thus, when William Blake deemed

Milton a member "of the Devil's party without knowing it," he opened the way to skeptical readers whose suspicions would find powerful support in the Freudian theory of the unconscious.[15] Milton's representation of Satan, especially in the opening books of *Paradise Lost* where his debts to Tasso's infernal council in canto 4 of the *Liberata* are also noteworthy, has prompted critics to suspect some division in his sympathies that receives no direct expression. According to such readings, symptoms of Miltonic ambivalence are inscribed in the vigor and alacrity of the author's own assertions to the contrary whenever the devil may appear to score a point in his own favor. The by-now-familiar Freudian paradox of "latent," as opposed to "manifest," content rationalizes these claims with varying degrees of success that depend on our own convictions about Milton's conscious control of his material and our enthusiasm for the methods of psychoanalysis. Stanley Fish, the contemporary leader of the counterattack against A. J. A. Waldock and other exponents of this skeptical vision of the deliberate artistry in *Paradise Lost*, has developed a theory of reading that simultaneously denies and incorporates the views of Milton's detractors by making their mistaken responses exactly what the poet himself both planned for and aimed to reform once he had thus flushed them out into the open.[16]

But previous readers like Waldock were more inclined to doubt the unqualified prevalence of executive control in any narrator and were also under the spell of neo-Aristotelian critiques of authorial commentary whether in post-Reformation epics or in modern novels.[17] Therefore, they saw Milton's frequent interjections and interpretive glosses upon the action of his poem both as symptoms of unacknowledged sympathies and as artistic flaws. There are, as I have mentioned before, Homeric and Virgilian precedents for apostrophes from the poet directly addressing his heroes and remarking emotionally upon dramatic circumstances in the action as it unfolds. Milton, however, extends this convention into much more open and sustained signals that aim to clarify his thematic concerns to his audience. For example, he promptly undercuts the compelling rhetoric of the leader of the fallen angels with such undisguisedly partisan addenda as the following:

86

So spake th'Apostate Angel, though in pain,
Vaunting aloud, but rackt with deep despair.
(1.125–26)

Such asides seem "unfair" in a variety of senses. Aesthetically, they obtrude upon the impression of a seamless mimesis, the essential norm of neo-Aristotelian narrative theory. But one suspects that they also violate a moral agenda implicit in such artistic values. To critics of this persuasion, Milton may seem to exert a kind of authorial tyranny over his characters by allowing a prejudicial omniscience to manipulate the reader's response by mere assertion and without the "objectivity" supposedly achieved through dramatic demonstration of a point.

This division among Miltonists leaves an inviting opening for comparative study to remind such scholars of some overlooked aspects of the Italian poetry that their author sought to employ and transcend. An acquaintance with the options from which Milton could choose in the models that he inherited from his Italian precursors can give us a truer sense of the creative fusion that he ultimately worked upon the diverse precedents set for him by Ariosto and Tasso. An understanding of this creative merger can thus serve as a telling gloss upon contemporary disputes of the sort that engaged Fish and Waldock and that have roots in major aspects of the reception of Milton's poem since Dryden, Johnson, and Blake. On the one hand, Milton could carry on the theoretical self-awareness that profoundly conditioned Tasso's most accomplished writing; and on the other, he could employ the broader license of Ariosto's poetic persona to make unmistakably clear his intention of taking liberties to the full extent that a "more heroic" argument entitled him. Indeed, he could venture the previously unattempted combination of these seemingly contradictory options and boldly theorize that gesture in a direct discourse such as the proem that opens book 9. Perhaps daring innovation like this seems hardly surprising, given Milton's characteristically decisive appropriations from the full range of the literary tradition that he stood to inherit. However, our forgetfulness of this rich legacy often needs a reminder of the opportunities that it afforded for imitation despite what might appear to be the theoretical foreclosure of some possibilities. Milton proved entirely able both to reopen such options as Tasso had tried to rule out and to explain the rationale for such a decision without equivocation.

Furthermore, this division among Miltonists reflects kindred complications in our historical responses to Tasso's writings that remain alive among us down to the present moment. Despite his imposing credentials as a literary genius, another aspect of Tasso's career regularly vies for a major share of the attention that his fame as a writer has secured for him. Tasso's stormy personal life has become the stuff of romantic legend indelibly recorded by such literary masters as Goethe, Byron, and Baudelaire;[18] and this brand of fascination with the poet's private troubles hardly betokens just a period phenomenon. Montaigne, Tasso's contemporary, describes their meeting in Ferrara as a vividly persuasive instance in his most devastating and sustained demonstration of the pretenses of human intelligence, the "Apology for Raymond Sebond":

> Countless minds have been ruined by their very power and suppleness. What a leap has just been taken, because of the very restlessness and liveliness of his mind, by one of the most judicious and ingenious of men, a man more closely molded by the pure poetry of antiquity than any other Italian poet has been for a long time! Does he not have reason to be grateful to that murderous vivacity of his mind? to that brilliance that has blinded him? to that exact and intent apprehension of his reason, which has deprived him of reason? to the careful and laborious pursuit of the sciences, which has led him to stupidity? to that rare aptitude for the exercises of the mind, which has left him without exercise and without mind? I felt even more vexation than compassion to see him in Ferrara in so piteous a state, surviving himself, not recognizing himself or his works, which, without his knowledge, and yet before his eyes, have been brought out uncorrected and shapeless.[19]

The bitter and persistent irony in Montaigne's series of rhetorical questions can serve to highlight the skepticism that has haunted Tasso's renown from almost the very moment that his literary accomplishments began to attract widespread attention.

Montaigne's insistent notice of the dark side of human genius emphasizes the severe limitations that disqualify our grander senses of ourselves from any undisputed exaltation; and it stands in startling contrast to the nobler images of our nature and the promise of human potential often celebrated in the traditional notion of the Renaissance. Compare, for instance, Tasso's own idea of the poet's role as he conceived it not even two decades prior to Montaigne's record of his impressions of the Tasso whom he actually encountered in Ferrara; for it was when the young poet had finished somewhat less than a quarter of the epic that assures his fame, *Gerusalemme liberata*, that he paused to theorize, in *Discorsi dell'arte poetica*, about the nature of the enterprise that then engaged him. In the process, he portrayed the maker of heroic poetry as a God-like creator who imitates the Author of us all in his capacity as a creative artist. "An excellent poet," as Tasso described him, "is called divine for no other reason except that by working like the supreme Artificer he comes to share his divinity."[20]

Tasso's exalted self-image and high-minded intentions are sometimes belied in the results of his efforts; and this perception authorizes the image of him as both an exemplary disaster of overreaching intellectualism, such as Montaigne puts forward, and a victim of courtly intrigue and other adversities of fate, such as romantic legend maintains. Current versions of these proclivities depend upon psychoanalytic theory, and they are duly balanced by responses that give greater credit to Tasso's stated ambitions as a poet-theorist who repeatedly elaborated rationales for his artistic endeavors that can help us to assess his accomplishments. The translations that follow are an effort to make such judgments more fully informed than has been possible heretofore, especially for readers without Italian. They are not foolproof guides to the mysteries of the *Liberata* nor magic keys to the psyche of its troubled author; however, they do provide clues that can assist a wide range of readers in the varied processes of literary detection and analysis.

For example, when an accomplished Freudian respondent like Margaret Ferguson cites *Discorsi del poema eroico* because it "provides a particularly interesting gloss on Tasso's defense of

Bernardo [his father] and the ethical dilemmas which confront him [Torquato] as he tries to play the three somewhat incompatible roles of poet, orator, and philosopher devoted to truth,"[21] a glance at the passage under review as it first appeared in *Discorsi dell'arte poetica* is informative. There Tasso is addressing the same material, which includes the Oedipal dilemma of patricide.[22] Naturally, a psychoanalytic reader is attracted to such a topic because of its crucial relationship to an essential Freudian theory; but its presence in a cinquecento poetics directly inspired by Aristotle's brief treatise of the same kind would seem less revealing to a reader with a different agenda, especially when he recalls that Sophocles' tragedy is the central proof-text of Tasso's model theorist and thus a likely citation in any example he might give. Further, a reader familiar with the early *Discorsi* would note at this juncture in that text (which Tasso expanded and revised to create the gloss cited by Ferguson) that its author originally was not trying simultaneously to play three incompatible roles. Rather, he was *distinguishing* between two roles, that of the poet and the orator, in order to stress their difference, perhaps even their incompatability, in regard to their representation of material like patricide.

Since his perspective ultimately derives from clinical studies of mental illness, a Freudian critic is likely to discover psychopathology with some regularity, no matter what the evidence may suggest to the contrary; yet one must admit that this passage provides an especially tempting occasion for someone of that persuasion. However, Tasso's initial reflections on this subject also take place at a particular historical moment in his career, when grand plans were in the making and subsequent controversies unforeseeable. Thus, whatever intrapsychic revelations we may be inclined to extract from the passage cited by Ferguson should be tempered by an awareness of their author's unpredictable evolution as a literary theorist and his unanticipated emergence into public debate over such issues. The conflicts within his personality probably have definite correlations to those of the social environment that he inhabited; and the Oedipal model of Freudian psychoanalysis thus requires considerable revision, if not abandonment, in the light of such public developments.

To give Ferguson her due, she does acknowledge that "the temporality of ghost-killing is complex" and that history, as well as Tasso's critics, "had provided a script in which the notion of 'first things first' was highly problematic."[23] The elements of conflict and paradox in Tasso's career abound; and whatever its potentially systemic biases, psychoanalysis often encounters such troublesome obstacles with honesty and courage. This unwillingness to gloss over struggle and contradiction amounts to the prime virtue of a Freudian viewpoint, even though it sometimes imports such elements into places where their presence beforehand was questionable.

The translations that follow offer the reader a chance to sample Tasso's own reflections about narrative as they evolved during the writing of the *Liberata*. I wish that they included his letters from the same period; but that would require at least another volume and Herculean labors of editing, since the last effort at a comprehensive publication of Tasso's *epistolario* dates to the mid-nineteenth century and stands in need of extensive revision.[24] In these documents the full play of strife and irresolution in the poet's reflections is most thoroughly visible, as are his moments of clarity and his decisive syntheses of potentially conflicting options. A mere selection from their number could easily misrepresent the range of attitudes toward his own work that Tasso entertained.

Michael Murrin's defense of the allegorical integrity of Tasso's poem exerts a powerful appeal through just such a process, but its accounting for divergent tendencies thus falls inevitably short. He and Ferguson represent poles between which readers of Tasso may navigate to acquire an overall appreciation of his masterwork. Efforts to reduce the distance between their points of vantage warrant attention but sometimes entail overly reductive approximations. Thus, when Timothy Hampton attempts to reconcile his reading of Tasso's development with that of Ferguson, he notes that she

> suggests that the poet's revision of his poem constitutes the working out of a psychic struggle in which the paternal superego is embraced and the self turns back to repress the introjected

91

maternal ego. I read the shift as an attempt to forestall the dangers of reading and to fix, or at least control, the ambiguities inherent in both exemplarity and poetic language. These two perspectives can be seen as essentially parallel if we recall the work of recent feminist critics, who link the authority of patriarchy to the control of linguistic play.[25]

Such deft harmonizations of rival viewpoints may merely depend on what we choose to recall. From certain altitudes everything looks pretty much the same—though the higher we ascend, the more we see of less and less. In the course of the theorizing covered by the following translations, Tasso himself moved from a central concern with the structural unity of his epic's plot to a strategic desire to assert the thematic coherence of its allegorical import; and if we disregard the evidence of a few letters, he managed the transit rather smoothly. Interpreters ultimately base their readings upon theories and texts that help them to sustain their favorite arguments, and selective oversight of alternative responses inevitably plays its part in this process. In "Allegoria del poema" Tasso, I suggest, became the first—and perhaps the most perceptive—misreader of the *Liberata*. To deserve that title, he had to overlook earlier ambitions or to subordinate them emphatically for a moment; and whatever misprision occurs in that prefatory document may in part be due to the dynamics of intrapsychic conflict or to the exigencies of reception by a given audience. Like Hampton, I incline toward the latter explanation, while finding (as he does) that they are by no means mutually exclusive. However, the translations that follow are offered to allow contemporary interpreters without Italian a closer look at some of the changes that Tasso went through in arriving at that allegorical vision of his own epic. Such readers may thereby arrive, better informed, at their own vision of Tasso's shifting perspectives upon his heroic project in its most enduring form, *Gerusalemme liberata*.

Translations

Torquato Tasso to
His Readers

Gentle readers, since no human action was ever perfect in every aspect, it does not seem unusual to me that none has ever lacked its detractors. Therefore, when I began this work[1] that now comes into your hands and when I prepared to print it, I clearly foresaw that there would be someone, or rather many, who would condemn both of my decisions. They would consider it inappropriate for a person who resides in Padova in order to pursue legal studies to spend time on such matters; and they would consider it most inappropriate for a youth of my age, which has not yet reached nineteen years, to presume so far beyond himself as to dare to submit his first efforts to the view of men to be judged by so great a range of opinions.

Nonetheless, I feel impelled by my genius, which inclines more toward poetry than anything else, and by the encouragement of the most esteemed Messer Danese Cattaneo, who excels no less in writing than in sculpture. Being further confirmed in this opinion by Messer Cesare Pavesi, a gentleman worthy of great praise both in poetry and in the more serious literature of philosophy, I dared to apply myself to this endeavor even though I knew that it would displease my father; for due both to his long life and to the many and varied concerns that have passed through his hands, he knows the instability of fortune and the mutability of present times. Thus, he would have wanted me to pay greater attention to more practical studies whereby I would have been able to acquire what he gained as a poet and, much more, as an envoy to princes; and then, having gained it, he lost it through the malignity of his lot and has not yet been able to recover it. Having so solid a background as a knowledge of law, I would not have to face the difficulties that he sometimes faced.

But since I received the encouragement of many friends and since my natural inclination—the desire to make myself well known (which perhaps occurs more easily through writing poetry than through practicing law)—had greater influence upon me, I began to act upon my idea, trying all the while to keep it hidden from my father. But I had not progressed very far toward that goal which I had proposed to myself before he was well aware of my plan; and although it weighed heavily upon him, he still decided in the end to let me run where my youthful enthusiasm was carrying me. Thus, as Signor Tomasso Lomellino, a most esteemed gentleman of the finest character, and many others can attest, I brought this poem to a conclusion in a space of ten months; and upon showing it to the most distinguished Signor Molino and Signor Veniero, whose worth far exceeds their very great fame, I was warmly encouraged by them to have it published. One can see a letter written about this matter by the aforementioned Signor Veniero to my father, who, without the authority and opinion of these most learned and judicious gentlemen, would not have given me his permission in this, even though he was first told about it by Danese and Pavese, whose judgment he especially valued when he had only seen a part of my work.

My *Rinaldo* thus comes forth to present itself for your inspection, protected by the shield of such authorities from any malicious attacks. Gentle readers, I ask you to be willing to consider it as the offspring of a young man, who, if he sees that this, his first effort, pleases you, will try one day to give you something more worthy of coming into your hands that can gain him greater praise. I believe it will not bother you that, departing somewhat from the way of the moderns, I have rather wished to draw near to those better ancient poets; however, you will not find me bound to the most severe laws of Aristotle, which have often rendered those poems less pleasant that otherwise would have been most pleasant to you. But I have only followed those precepts of his which will not take away your delight, like the frequent use of episodes, and the elimination of the poet's personal voice by introducing others to speak, and the effecting of recognitions and reversals through either necessary or verisimilar causes, and the appropriate expression of customs and diction.

Indeed, it is true that in ordering[2] my poem I have labored even more to make sure that the plot has unity—if not strictly so, at least when considered overall. Some parts may appear inessential and not such that if they were removed, the whole would be destroyed as, when one takes away a member from the human body, it becomes maimed and incomplete. Yet these parts are such that if not each one by itself, at least they all together have no small effect, like that made by the scalp, beard, and other body hair: if one of them is taken away, no apparent harm is done; but if many are removed, the body becomes very ugly and disfigured.[3] But I would like my works to be judged not by the strict followers of Aristotle, who have before their eyes the perfect example of Virgil and Homer and who never attend to delight and to what today's customs require, nor by those overly enamored of Ariosto. For the former would not concede that any poem was worthy of praise in which some part had no apparent effect and, if removed, would not ruin the whole, even though there are many such parts in the *Furioso* and the *Amadigi* and some such parts in the ancient Greeks and Latins. And the latter severely reprehend me for not using those proems and moral sentiments that Ariosto always employs—and all the more because even my father, a man whose authority and value the world knows, sometimes let himself be carried away by this convention.

But, on the other hand, neither the prince of poets, Virgil, nor Homer, nor the other ancient poets used them; and Aristotle clearly states in his *Poetics* (which the most eloquent Sigonio is now expounding in Padova with glory for himself and wonder and envy from others) that the more a poet imitates, the better a poet he is, and he imitates more, the less he speaks as a poet and the more he introduces others to speak. Danese well observed this precept in his poem composed in imitation of the ancients and according to the way shown by Aristotle, which Danese still encourages me to follow. But those who speak all

97

the moral sentiments and proverbs in the person of the poet have not yet observed Aristotle, nor have those who speak in the person of the poet only in the beginning of the cantos. Beyond the fact that by doing this they do not imitate, it seems that they are likewise lacking in imagination; for they do not know to place such things elsewhere than in the beginning of the canto. Since, to some, this could seem excessive ambition to show oneself learned or even, through joking, to be held pleasing and witty by the crowd, perhaps it is not without affectation. In this regard I believe what the most learned Signor Pigna said is true: that Ariosto would not have fashioned such proems if he had not thought that, dealing with various knights and various actions and often abandoning one subject and picking up another again, it was sometimes necessary to appease his audience, which is almost always done in those proems by proposing what ought to be considered in the canto and by joining those things which are to be said with those that have already been said. And the same reason, besides convention, moved my father to imitate him.

But since I consider one single knight, restricting all his deeds to one action (so far as present tastes allow), and since I have woven my poem with an uninterrupted and continuous thread, I do not know why I should use such proems, especially since I see my opinion is confirmed by Veniero, Molino, and [Bernardo] Tasso—persons whose authority could convince anybody. Further, I know that this had first been the opinion of Sperone, a man who entirely understands the arts and sciences. Therefore, do not be displeased to see my *Rinaldo* composed in part as an imitation of the ancients and in part as an imitation of the moderns.

Discourses on the
Art of Poetry

Discourse 1

Whoever proposes to write a heroic poem must attend to three matters: choosing a subject able to accommodate the most excellent form that the poet's artistry will aim to give it; giving it this form; and, finally, adorning it with the most exquisite ornaments appropriate to its nature. This whole discourse, then, will divide itself under those three headings that I have specified.[1] Beginning with the judgment that the poet must show in selecting a subject, I will pass on to the art that he must sustain, first in setting it forth and shaping it, then in trimming and adornment.

That which has not yet received any touch of the orator's or the poet's artistry is called the raw material, and it comes under the poet's consideration in the same way that iron or wood comes under the craftsman's. So, just as the shipwright is obliged not only to know what the form of ships should be but also to recognize what sort of wood is most suited in itself to take on this form, it likewise behooves the poet not only to possess the skill to give form to his subject but also the judgment to recognize it. And he must choose one, by its very nature, capable of every refinement.

The raw material is almost always given to the orator by chance or by necessity; it comes to the poet by choice. Therefore, it sometimes happens that what is improper for the poet is laudable in the orator. The poet is taxed for exciting pity for a character who has voluntarily stained his hands in his father's blood; the orator, however, may arouse pity at the same event

99

and gain the highest praise. The former's choice is censured while necessity excuses the latter and his ingenuity is praised. So, just as there is no doubt that the power of art can in some ways do violence to the nature of the subject—making those things appear lifelike that are not so in themselves and those things pitiable that would cause no pity on their own and those things wondrous that would stir no wonder—there is, as well, no doubt that these effects are achieved more easily, and at a higher level, in those subjects already disposed to accommodate them.

Suppose that, with identical artistry and with identical eloquence, one person wants to portray the pathos of Oedipus, who, through simple ignorance, killed his father; and another wants to portray the pathos of Medea, who, quite well aware of her wickedness, slaughtered her children.[2] The plot contrived from the experiences of Oedipus will achieve much greater pathos than that based upon the fate of Medea. The former will inflame the feelings of pity; the latter will scarcely prove capable of warming them up, even though the artistry employed in both be not only similar but equal. In like manner a signet of the same form does its job much better in wax than in another substance more fluid or more firm; and a marble or a golden statue is more prized than one of wood or of a less noble stone, even though the efforts of Phidias or Praxiteles are equally visible in both. It is well to have touched on this so that we know how much the choice of one subject, rather than another, matters to the epic. It remains for us to see whence the subject should be drawn.

The material, which may as happily be termed the subject, either is invented (and then it seems that the poet takes part not only in the choice but in the invention as well) or is drawn from chronicles of history. In my opinion, however, material taken from chronicles is much the better, since the epic poet must try for versimilitude in every part of his poem (I assume this as a well-established principle); and it is not verisimilar that an illustrious action, such as those in an heroic poem, would not have been written down and passed on to the memory of posterity with the help of history. Great events cannot go unknown; and when they are not recorded in writing, people claim them false on this ground alone. Considering them false, people do not so easily consent to being moved now to wrath, now to terror, now to pity—or to being, by turns, delighted, saddened, held in suspense or in rapture. In sum, they do not follow the sequence of events with the same expectation and delight as they would if they deemed that sequence true, either wholly or in part.

On this account, the poet must trick his readers with the appearance of truth. He must not merely persuade them that the things he has written are true; he must also suggest them to their senses in such a way that they do not believe that they are reading but, rather, that they are present and they see and hear them.[3] Thus, it is necessary to achieve in their minds this sense of truth, and the authority of history usually accomplishes this. I am speaking now of those poets who imitate illustrious actions, like the tragedian and the epic poet. The comic poet, imitator of base and common actions, may always invent his theme at will without undermining verisimilitude since no accounting of private actions is kept even among people who inhabit the same city. And though we read in Aristotle's *Poetics*[4] that people are usually pleased by the novelty of invented stories—e.g., Agathon's *Flower* among the ancients and, among us, the heroic tales of Boiardo and Ariosto and the tragic ones of some more recent writers—we should not let ourselves be persuaded that any invented story in a heroic poem deserves much praise, as the argument from verisimilitude proves and many others firmly establish from other premises.

Besides all these arguments, one may say that the poem's novelty does not principally consist in the subject's being invented and unheard of before but in the novelty of the plot's crisis and its resolution. Different ancients treated the stories of Thyestes and Medea and Oedipus; but, by arranging them differently, they successfully appropriated and renewed them. Therefore, that poem will be new whose complications and resolutions of plot are new and whose intermittent episodes are new, even though the subject is very well known and has been treated by others before. Conversely, that poem whose characters and plot are new cannot be called new when the poet develops and

101

resolves them in ways that others have before. Such are some modern tragedies whose subject and characters are invented but whose fabric is woven and unwoven just as it was among the ancient Greeks. They lack, therefore, both the authority that history brings with it and the novelty that invention seems to produce.

Therefore, the theme of an epic must be taken from chronicles of history. History, however, either involves a religion that we deem false or a religion that we believe true, like Christianity today and Judaism in the past. I do not think that the deeds of the Gentiles [i.e., pagans] offer us a subject suitable to make into a perfect epic because, in such poems, we sometimes want to refer to the deities worshipped by the Gentiles, or we do not want to. If we do not make such reference, the poem will lack wonder; if we do, it will lack verisimilitude in that part. Truly, that poem delights us little that does not include those wonders which so move the minds not only of the ignorant but of the intelligent, as well. I am speaking of those enchanted rings and shields, those flying steeds, those ships turned into nymphs, those phantoms that intervene between combatants, and other such things.[5] With these the judicious writer should season his poem as with spices because he thereby prompts and entices the appetite of the common people not only without the annoyance but with the pleasure, as well, of the most discerning. However, since natural power cannot effect such miracles, we must resort to supernatural power; and when we resort to the gods of the Gentiles, verisimilitude ends because what our people deem not only false but impossible cannot be verisimilar to them. And it is impossible that things so far beyond nature and humankind should proceed from the power of insubstantial and vain idols that do not exist and never did. Reading those poems based upon the errors of ancient religion, anyone of moderate intelligence can easily realize not only how far the wonder (if it warrants such a name) caused by Joves and Apollos and other Gentile godheads lies from verisimilitude but also how cold, dull, and ineffective it is.

These two qualities, the wondrous and the verisimilar, are exceedingly different, Signor Scipione.[6] Indeed, they are so dif-

102

ferent that they are nearly contrary to each other. Still, both one and the other are necessary in the epic poem. It requires, however, the skill of an excellent poet to join them together; and, though many have done so thus far, no one, to my knowledge, has taught how it is done. In fact, some men of the highest learning, seeing the tension between these two qualities, have decided that the verisimilar parts of poems are not wondrous and the wondrous parts not verisimilar but that since both are still necessary, one must advance the verisimilar at one time and the wondrous at another, in such a way that one does not succumb to the other but, rather, modulates it. For myself, I hold the opinion that no part should be found in a poem that is not verisimilar; and the reason that compels me to such a belief is as follows.

Poetry, in essence, is nothing other than imitation; this cannot be doubted.[7] And imitation cannot be dissociated from verisimilitude, since imitation means nothing more than making a likeness or a similitude. Therefore, no part of poetry excludes verisimilitude. Finally, verisimilitude is not one of those conditions requisite in poetry for greater beauty and adornment; it is proper to its essence, intrinsic, and more necessary than any other thing in any other part of it.[8] Still, although I hold the epic poet to the constant obligation of sustaining verisimilitude, I do not, therefore, disallow him from the other aspect, that is, the wondrous. Rather, I consider that one and the same action can be both wondrous and verisimilar; and many, I believe, are the ways of joining together such discordant qualities. The present requires discussing one of these, leaving the others for that part where we shall consider plot structure,[9] which is their proper place.

Some works that greatly exceed the power of men the poet attributes to God, to His angels, to demons, or to those granted such power by God or by demons, like saints and wizards and fairies. If considered by themselves, these works seem wondrous; in fact, common usage calls them miracles. These same works, if attention is given to the virtue and the power that have wrought them, are deemed verisimilar. Since our people have imbibed this opinion in the cradle, along with their milk, and

103

since it was confirmed in them by the masters of our blessed Faith (that is, that God and his ministers and demons and magicians, with his permission, can do things wondrous beyond the forces of nature) and, finally, since everyday they read and hear new examples related, therefore it does not appear to them beyond verisimilitude. Indeed, they not only believe it possible but think it has happened many times and can happen many times again. Likewise, to the ancients, who lived in the errors of their vain religion, those miracles must not have seemed impossible which not only the poets but sometimes the historians relate about their gods—for even if learned men deem them impossible (as they were), the opinion of the multitude suffices the poet in this, as in many other things; and many times, abandoning the exact truth of things, he is accustomed to, and should, hold closely to this opinion. In sum, one and the same action can be both wondrous and verisimilar: it is wondrous considered in itself and circumscribed by natural limits; it is verisimilar considered free from these limits, in its cause, which is supernatural, powerful, and wont to work similar wonders.

Those poems where Gentile deities are introduced lack this method of joining the verisimilar with the wondrous, whereas those poets who base their poetry on our religion can readily take advantage of it. In my judgment, this argument alone proves that the subject of an epic must be drawn from Christian and Hebrew history, not from Gentile history. Add to this that our religion brings with it—in heavenly and infernal councils, as well as in prophecies and rituals—such grandeur, such dignity, and such majesty as Gentile religion does not offer. And, finally, I do not know why whoever wishes to invest the idea of the perfect knight with form—as some modern writers seem to have intended—should deny him praise for piety and religion and figure him as impious and idolatrous. If the zeal of the true religion cannot, without manifest incongruence, be attributed to Theseus or Jason or others like them, abandon Theseus and Jason and the others and choose, instead, Charlemagne, Arthur, and their like. I shall pass over, for the moment, the poet's need to attend closely to improvement—if not inasmuch as he is a poet (for, as a poet, this is not his purpose), at least inasmuch as he is a citizen and part of the republic—and also that he will much better fire the minds of our people with the example of faithful knights than of infidels, because the example of the familiar and similar always moves us more than that of the strange and different.

The epic poet, thus, must take his theme from the history of a religion held true by us. But either such histories are so sacred and venerable that it is impiety to change them (the establishment of our Faith being based upon them), or they are not so holy as to contain an article of faith within them and thus do allow some things to be added, some removed, and others changed without the sin of impudence or irreligion. The epic poet will not dare reach his hand toward histories of the first kind; rather, he will leave them, in their pure and simple truth, for the pious, because invention here is not permitted. Furthermore, whoever invents nothing and, in effect, binds himself to a particular content would not be a poet but a historian. The theme of an epic, therefore, should be taken from chronicles of true religion but not of such great authority as to be unalterable.

Histories, moreover, contain events either of our times, or of times remote, or events neither very modern nor very ancient. History of distant eras affords the poet great leeway for invention. Since those things are so buried in the depths of antiquity that hardly a weak and hazy memory of them remains, the poet can change them again and again, at will, and recount them as he pleases without any consideration of the truth. With this leeway, however, comes a not-insignificant difficulty, because, along with ancient times, he must include ancient customs in his poem. But the greater portion of people of our time cannot read of that manner of warfare or armament used by the ancients, as well as nearly all their customs, without irritation; and one experiences this even in the books of Homer, which, although they are indeed divine, seem nonetheless annoying. Antiquated customs cause this for the main part; they are considered unacceptable, avoided as base, and held in disdain by those who have developed a taste for the gentility and decorum of the modern age. But whoever would introduce modern customs into ancient times might seem like an ill-advised painter who portrayed the figure of Cato or Cincinnatus dressed in the style of the youth of Milan or Naples or who dressed Hercules in a crested helmet and flowing cloak and took away his club and lion skin.

Modern history provides great convenience in this matter concerning customs and usage. It removes, however, nearly all freedom for invention, which is essential for poets and, particularly, for epic poets; for it would seem brazen daring in a poet to choose to describe the undertakings of Charles V otherwise than many who are alive today have witnessed and conducted them. Men cannot tolerate deception in those things that they know firsthand or those that they learned through the trustworthy accounts of fathers or grandfathers. But histories of times neither very modern nor very ancient do not entail the annoyance of outmoded customs nor deprive us of freedom for invention. Such are the times of Charlemagne and Arthur and those which either preceded or succeeded them by a little; and thus it happens that they have supplied innumerable romancers with subjects for poetic composition. The memory of these ages is not so fresh that any falsehood in relating them would seem impudence; further, their customs are not different from ours; and even if they are somewhat so, the practice of our poets has made them natural and familiar. Therefore, let the subject of an epic poem be taken from the history of true religion (but not so sacred as to be unchangeable) and from a time not very distant from, nor very near to, the memory of those now living.

Signor Scipione, I believe that all these conditions are required in the raw material, but not so much so that it cannot be made to assume the form of a heroic poem if it lacks a single one of them. Each alone has its effect—some more, some less—but all of them taken together matter so much that the subject is incapable of perfection without them. Still, beyond all these conditions required in an epic, I will add another one that is fundamentally necessary: that is, that the actions that must undergo the epic poet's artistry be noble and illustrious. This condition constitutes the nature of the epic; and in this, tragic and epic poetry correspond, and they differ from comedy, which imitates lowly actions. However, since it appears to be a common belief that tragedy and epic do not diverge in the things

106

imitated (for both imitate grand and illustrious actions) and that their generic divergence arises, rather, from a difference in the mode of imitation, it will be well to examine this matter in greater detail.

In his *Poetics*, Aristotle posits three essential and (let us say) generic differences by which one poem is separated and distinguished from another.[10] These are differences in the things imitated, in the mode of imitation, and in the instruments of imitation. The things are the actions. The mode is narration or representation: narration, when the person of the poet appears; representation, when the poet's person is effaced and those of the actors appear. The instruments are speech, harmony, and rhythm. Rhythm means the measure of movements and gestures discernible in the actors. Once Aristotle has established these three essential differences, he inquires how the determination of the genres of poetry proceeds from them. He says that tragedy and comedy agree in mode of imitation and in instruments, since each represents and employs, besides verse, rhythm and harmony. However, the difference in actions imitated distinguishes their natures: tragedy imitates noble actions, comedy ignoble actions. The epic, then, corresponds with tragedy in the things imitated, each of them imitating illustrious actions. But the mode of imitation distinguishes them: the epic poet narrates; the tragic poet represents. And the instruments of imitation distinguish them further: the epic poet employs verse alone while, besides verse, the tragic poet employs rhythm and harmony.

For these reasons, as Aristotle expressed them with that puzzling compression peculiar to him, the tragedian and the epic poet are believed to correspond entirely in the things that they imitate. I do not judge this to be true, although it is a common and universally held opinion; and the reason that leads me to this opinion is as follows. If epic and tragic actions shared the same nature, they would cause the same effects, since the same effects derive from the same causes. However, when they do not produce the same effects, it follows that their natures are different. And it is manifestly clear that the same effects do not proceed from tragedy and epic. Tragic actions arouse terror and

107

pity,[11] and they are no longer tragic when terror and pity are missing. Epics, however, did not originate to move either terror or pity, nor was this condition required in them as necessary. If sometimes terrible or pitiful misfortunes appear in heroic poems, one does not, therefore, look for terror and pity throughout the whole fabric of the tale. Such fortunes are accidental in it and merely decorative. Therefore, if we call the actions of tragedy and epic equally illustrious, their illustriousness is of different natures. Tragic illustriousness consists of the unexpected and sudden change of fortune and the magnitude of the events that arouse terror and pity. Heroic illustriousness, however, is based on undertakings of exalted martial valor and on deeds of courtesy, generosity, piety, and religion. Such actions, appropriate for epic, in no way suit tragedy. Thus, it follows that the characters introduced into either epic or tragedy differ in nature, even if they are of royal state and supreme dignity in both forms. Tragedy requires characters neither good nor wicked but of moderate virtue, such as Orestes, Electra, and Jocasta.[12] Since Aristotle discovered this moderate virtue more in Oedipus than in any other, he judged his character better suited for tragic plots than any other. Epic, however, needs the highest virtues, which are called heroic due to their heroic virtue. The epitome of piety appears in Aeneas, of martial courage in Achilles, of prudence in Ulysses—and (to come to our times) of loyalty in Amadis, of constancy in Bradamante.[13] Indeed, the sum of all these virtues appears in some of these characters. Even if the tragedian and the epic poet sometimes take the same character as the subject of their works, they regard him variously and from different angles. In Hercules and Theseus, the epic poet considers their valor and their excellence in arms; the tragedian considers them guilty of some fault and, thereby, fallen into misery. Epic poets, furthermore, treat not only the height of virtue but also excess of vice with much less risk than tragedians usually do. Mezentius and Marganorre and Archeloro are examples of this, as could be Busiris, Procrustes, Diomedes, and others like them.[14]

It can be shown from what has been said that the difference between tragedy and epic does not alone derive from the differ-

ence of instruments and the mode of imitation but much more—
and much more basically—from the difference in the things
imitated. This difference is more immediate, more intrinsic, and
more essential than the others. If Aristotle did not mention this,
it is because, in that place, it was enough for him to show that
tragedy and epic differ; and this is satisfactorily demonstrated
by those other two differences which, at first sight, appear much
more noteworthy. This illustriousness, however, which we have
established as fundamental to heroic poetry, can be more or less
illustrious; thus, a subject will be the more suitable for the most
excellent form of the epic inasmuch as it contains events more
noble and more lofty within itself. So, although I do not deny
that less magnificent events—like the loves of Florio and those
of Theagenes and Characlea[15]—can be composed into an epic,
nonetheless, in this idea of the most perfect epic which we are
presently exploring, it is necessary that the subject in itself be of
the first rank of nobility and of excellence. Aeneas' coming to
Italy has such stature; for this subject, besides being lofty and
illustrious in itself, is most lofty and illustrious considering that
the Roman Empire originated in that coming. The divine poet
paid particular attention to this, as he indicates in the opening of
the *Aeneid*:

Tantae molis erat Romanam condere gentem.
(1.33)

So great a task it was to found the race of Rome.

The liberation of Italy from subjection to the Goths, which
provided Trissino the subject for his epic, has equal stature:
such are those deeds which were happily and gloriously exe-
cuted either for the dignity of the Empire or for the exaltation of
the Christian faith. They capture by themselves the minds of the
readers, and they awaken expectation and incredible delight.
Add to them the artistry of an excellent poet and nothing in the
human mind is outside their power.

These, then, Signor Scipione, are the conditions a judicious
poet must seek in the raw material. To review them, briefly:

109

historical authority, true religion, freedom of invention, a suitably flexible period in time, events of grandeur and nobility. However, what we call the subject, before it undergoes the epic poet's artistry, becomes, after the poet arranges and adjusts it, the plot; and it is no longer simply the subject but the form and soul of the poem. Aristotle judged it so;[16] and we consider it at least a blend of subject and form, if it is not purely form. In the beginning of this discourse, however, we compared what we have come to call the raw material with what natural philosophers call primary matter. Just as these philosophers, in considering primary matter (entirely without form though it is), nonetheless take account of its size, which is its constant and eternal attribute, evident before the birth of form and remaining after form decays, so the poet, likewise, should attend to the size of his subject; for when choosing any subject for treatment, he must choose it together with a certain size, this consideration being inseparably a part of it. Let him beware, then, lest he select a size so great that while shaping the plot structure, if he wants to introduce numerous episodes and to adorn and heighten events by nature commonplace, the poem grows to such magnitude as seems gross and excessive; for an epic poem must not exceed a certain fixed magnitude, as we will discuss in its place. So, if he would avoid this grossness and excess, he will have to abandon digressions and other ornaments necessary to the poem and confine himself almost completely to the plain and simple terms of historical fact.

This appears to have happened to Lucan and Silius Italicus, for both one and the other embraced subjects too ample and abundant: the former undertook to treat not only the Battle of Pharsalia (as the title indicates) but the whole civil war between Caesar and Pompey; and the latter the whole Second Punic War.[17] These subjects, so vast in themselves, were able to occupy the whole extent allotted to the magnitude of the epic, leaving no place for the poet's ingenuity and invention. And often, when comparing the same events as treated by Silius the poet and the historian Livy, they seem to me much plainer and less adorned in the poet than in the historian—exactly contrary to what the nature of these things requires. One can observe the same thing in Trissino, who wanted the whole expedition of Belisarius against the Goths as the subject of his poem and, therefore, is often sparer and drier than becomes a poet. If he had chosen to describe only one—and that the most noble— part of that campaign, perhaps his poem would have turned out lovelier and more adorned with beautiful inventions. In sum, whoever proposes too vast a subject for himself is constrained to extend his poem beyond the suitable limit; or, at least, he is forced to abandon the episodes and other ornaments that are most necessary to the poet. (And perhaps this excessive length appears in *Orlando innamorato* and *Orlando furioso* to whoever considers these two books, distinct in title and author, as almost a single poem—which, in effect, they are.)

Homer's judgment was exceptional in this regard: having proposed himself a slight subject and expanded it with episodes and enriched it with every other sort of ornament, he then reduced it to laudable and seemly size. Virgil proposed himself a somewhat larger subject, as though to gather into a single poem as much as Homer contained in two; he did not, however, select a subject of such size that he was compelled to succumb to either of those two errors. Still, he sometimes proceeds in a manner so restrained and so sparing of ornament that despite that marvelous and matchless simplicity and concision of his, he lacks, perchance, Homer's rich and eloquent abundance. In this regard, I remember Speroni,[18] whose private study I used to frequent as a student in Padua, no less often and no less willingly than the public schools, since it seemed to me a replica of that Academy and Lyceum where the Socratic and Platonic philosophers used to hold their discussions.[19] I recall his saying that our Latin poet was more like the Greek orator [Demosthenes] than was the Greek poet and that our Latin orator [Cicero] more resembled the Greek poet than did the Greek orator; for the Greek orator and poet each exclusively pursued that virtue proper to his art, whereas their Latin counterparts had each expropriated that excellence proper to the other's art. And, truly, whoever wishes to examine closely the style of each of them will see that Cicero's abundant eloquence is most similar to Homer's breadth of fluency, just as Demosthenes and Virgil

111

are much alike in the sharpness, density, and vigor of a remarkable concision.

To review, then, what has been said: the size of the raw material must be great enough (but no greater) to be able to accommodate considerable addition from the poet's artistry without exceeding the limits of appropriate magnitude. However, now that we have discussed the judgment that a poet must show in choosing a subject, order requires that we treat, in the following discourse, the art with which he must shape and arrange it.

Discourse 2

After the poet has chosen a subject in itself capable of every refinement, there remains the other much more difficult task of giving it form and poetic arrangement. In this task, as in choosing a proper subject, nearly all the power of the art shows forth. But consideration of things as they should have been, not as they were, and regard for universal verisimilitude, rather than truth in the particulars, basically constitute and determine the nature of poetry and distinguish it from history. Therefore, the poet must first take note whether the subject he chooses to treat contains any event that would be more verisimilar or more wondrous if it happened otherwise or would give more delight for any other reason whatever. All such events that he finds—all events that could better have happened in another way—he may change at will, again and again, and with no respect for fact or history; and he may rearrange the accidents of history in the manner he deems best, combining complete fiction with doctored fact.

The divine Virgil knew very well how to apply this precept. Thus, he pursued what he judged best and most noteworthy, not what he believed true, in the wanderings of Aeneas as well as in the wars between him and Latinus. For, not only are the love and death of Dido and his stories of Polyphemus and of the Sybil and of Aeneas' descent into the underworld false, but he also describes the battles between Aeneas and the peoples of

Latium otherwise than they occurred according to the facts. This appears clearly by comparing his *Aeneid* with Livy's first book and with other historians. However, just as he so greatly distorted chronological order in the Dido episode to have occasion to mingle the most pleasant amorous discourse amid the harshness of the other matters and to assign a lofty and hereditary cause to the enmity between Romans and Carthaginians and just as he had recourse to the tale of Polyphemus and of the Sybil to combine the marvelous with the verisimilar, he likewise altered the death of Turnus, said nothing of that of Aeneas, introduced the death of Amata, and changed the events and the order of the clashes to increase Aeneas' glory and to bring his most noble poem to a more perfect conclusion. (Of course, the antiquity of the period also greatly favored these inventions.)

Poetic license, however, must not be extended so far that the poet dares to change completely the ultimate conclusion of the actions he chooses to treat or even of some of those principal and better-known incidents already accepted as true by popular report. He would display such audacity who described Rome as conquered and Carthage as conqueror or Hannibal as overcome by Fabius Maximus in the open field, not artfully kept at bay. Homer's audacity would be the same if that were true which some say falsely (though most suitably to their own purpose):

che i Greci rotti, e che Troia vittrice,
e che Penelopea fu meretrice.
(Ariosto, *Orlando furioso* 35.27.7–8)

that the Greeks were vanquished, and Troy was the victor, and Penelope was a whore.

This robs poetry of that authority which comes to it from history and which moved us to conclude that the theme of epic poetry must be based on some history. Let our epic poet leave the end and the beginning of the event, as well as some of the more illustrious deeds, either slightly changed or not at all changed from their own truth. Then, if he thinks best, let him change the means and the conditions of the other events; let him shift their timing and sequence; and, in sum, let him appear as an artful

113

poet, rather than a truthful historian. If, however, he finds certain events in the subject he has set himself that occur just as they should have, the poet can imitate them without changes, just as they are. He does not, thereby, shed the poet's mantle and don the historian's, since it can sometimes happen that two writers treat the same events—one as a poet, the other as an historian—but they regard them from different perspectives: the historian narrates them as true; the poet imitates them as verisimilar. And even though I do not believe Lucan is a poet, I am not prompted to this belief by the reason that leads others to believe so—that is, that he is not a poet because he narrates true events. This alone is not enough. He is not a poet, however, because he so binds himself to the truth of the particulars that he has no regard for universal verisimilitude; and even though he narrates the deeds as they were done, he does not take care to imitate them as they should have been done.

Now, once the poet has reduced the truth and particularity of history to verisimilitude and universality—which are essential to his art—let him take care with the plot. (I call the form of the poem, which may be defined as the fabric or composition of the events, the plot.)[20] Let him take care, I say, that the plot he would fashion from history be whole or, as we say, entire; that it be of suitable size; and that it be single.[21] I will discuss these three conditions necessary to the plot one at a time and in the order that I have set them.

The plot must be whole or entire because we expect perfection of it, and whatever is not whole cannot be perfect. This wholeness will be found in the plot if it has a beginning, a middle, and an end. The beginning is that which, by necessity, comes after nothing else; the other things come after it. The end is that which comes after the other things; nothing comes after it. The middle is situated between the beginning and the end; and it comes after some things and some things come after it. However, to go somewhat beyond the brevity of these definitions, I call that plot whole which contains in itself everything necessary for understanding it: the origin and causes of the event chosen as a subject are expressed; and it is brought, by the requisite means, to a conclusion that leaves nothing unfinished

114

or ill resolved. Boiardo's *Orlando innamorato* wants this condition of wholeness; nor does one find it in the *Furioso* of Ariosto. The *Innamorato* lacks an ending, and the *Furioso*, a beginning. Still, this was not an artistic failure in the former—rather, the fault of death; and in the latter, it was not unawareness but the choice to finish what his predecessor had started. That the *Innamorato* is incomplete requires no proof. It is equally clear that the *Furioso* is incomplete—for if we say Ruggiero's love is the main action of that poem, it lacks a beginning; and if we call the war between Charlemagne and Agramante the main action, it likewise lacks a beginning. For other than the indications of a line or two, we do not read in the text when or how Ruggiero fell in love with Bradamante nor when or how the Africans began to make war on the French. And readers many times would proceed benighted in their understanding of these plots if they did not take from the *Innamorato* what is necessary for their comprehension. Yet, as I have said, one must not consider *Orlando innamorato* and the *Furioso* as two distinct books but as a single poem, begun by the one poet and concluded by the other—who spun with the same yarn though he tied and dyed it better. Considering them this way, they become a whole poem that lacks nothing for the understanding of its plots.

Were it true that Homer took the Trojan War as theme for his poem, the *Iliad* would likewise lack this condition of wholeness. However, this opinion, which many of the ancients professed, has been disproved and confounded by the scholars of our century; and it appears clearly false. If Homer himself is a reliable witness of his own intentions, the wrath of Achilles, not the Trojan War, is sung of in the *Iliad*:

> Tell me, Muse, of the wrath of Peleus' son,
> Achilles, which brought to the Greeks endless woes
> And sent many heroic souls to hell.
>
> $(1.1-4)$[22]

All that is said of the Trojan War he intends as correlative and dependent on the wrath of Achilles and, finally, as episodes to enhance Achilles' glory and the grandeur of that plot. The origin and cause of his wrath are fully told in the coming of Chryses the priest and the taking of Briseis; and with a sustained purposefulness, his wrath is drawn to its conclusion—that is, the reconciliation of Achilles and Agamemnon, caused by the death of Patroclus. Therefore, that plot is everywhere perfect and holds, in the folds of its fabric, whole and perfect transparency and need not go a-begging elsewhere extra aids to understanding. One can, perhaps, criticize this fault in certain modern poems where one needs to resort to prefatory prose explanations—for whatever clarity is gained by prose arguments and other such devices is neither artful nor truly poetic; it is extrinsic and unearned.

Since we have adequately dealt with the first condition required of the plot, let us turn to the second, size. Although we already discussed size where we took up the choice of subject, it does not seem excessive or awkward to speak of it now while we consider the creation of form; for there we attended to the size that the raw material entails on its own; here we shall consider the size that the poem assumes under the poet's hand by means of the episodes.

Natural forms seek out a determined size, and they are circumscribed within fixed limits of more or less, which they may not violate in excess or defect. Artificial forms, likewise, seek out a determined magnitude. One could introduce the form of a ship neither into a grain of millet nor into the mass of Mount Olympus, for form is said to be introduced simultaneously with the natural and proper function of such form. However, the function of a ship, which is to plow the waves and conduct passengers from shore to shore, could never be found in a mass so excessive or so defective. And perhaps the nature of poems is like that. But I do not want to consider to what size the form of the heroic poem can grow; rather, I want to consider to what size it best should grow. And without doubt, it should be larger than tragic and comic plots are by nature.

Just as there may be elegance and grace in small bodies but never beauty and perfection, small epic poems may likewise be lovely and elegant, but not beautiful and perfect; for beyond proportion, size is necessary for beauty and perfection. This size, however, should not exceed acceptable limits, as in pic-

116

tures of Tityus "who, stretched out, covered seven fields."[23] But just as the eye is the right judge of comely stature in the body— for that body has suitable size whose sight does not confound the eye and whose proportions the eye can appraise, taking in all its members at a glance—so is the ordinary human memory the right index of the appropriate length of the epic. That poem is suitably large in which the memory does not darken or fail but, taking the whole in at once, can consider how one thing connects with another and depends on a third and how the parts are in proportion to themselves and to the whole. Without doubt, those poems are faulty, and the work spent on them in good part lost, in which the reader has barely passed the middle when he has forgotten the beginning. One loses the pleasure in a poem that must be assiduously pursued by the poet as its main perfection; that is, one loses the necessary or verisimilar succession of one event after another and how one thing is linked to another and inseparable from it and, in sum, how a natural and verisimilar and surprising dénouement results from a skillful interweaving of connections. And perhaps, to one who would consider the *Innamorato* and the *Furioso* as a single poem, its length could seem excessive and unlikely to be retained by an average memory after simply one reading.

Unity follows size and is the last condition that we attributed to the plot. This, Signor Scipione, is the issue in our times that has occasioned various and lengthy disputes among those "whom literary passion leads into battle."[24] While some have deemed unity necessary, others have believed, to the contrary, that a multitude of actions better suits the heroic poem—"*Et magno iudice se quisque tuetur.*"[25] Defenders of unity make themselves a shield of the authority of Aristotle and the majesty of ancient Greek and Latin poets without ignoring the arms reason supplies. However, their opponents counter with the customs of the present age and with the universal agreement of ladies and lords and the courts and (so it seems) with experience, as well—the infallible test of truth. They see that Ariosto, who abandoned the path of ancient writers and the rules of Aristotle and who embraced many and diverse actions in his poem, is read and reread by all ages and both sexes, known in all languages, liked and praised by all. He lives and, through his renown, forever lives again; and human tongues exalt his name. Trissino, on the other hand, who proposed to imitate the poems of Homer devoutly and to confine himself to the precepts of Aristotle, is mentioned by few, read by fewer, esteemed by almost no one, voiceless in the theater of the world and dead to human eyes. Scarcely a trace of him remains, buried in the library or study of some literary man.

Besides experience, there is no lack of solid and convincing arguments in favor of multiple plots; and some learned and ingenious men have sought out new and subtle reasons to strengthen and confirm them either because they believe them or because they want to display their intellectual power and gain favor in the world by serving popular opinion like a tyrant, which she truly is. Even though I hold such men in the highest esteem for learning and eloquence, I myself still think that Ariosto should not be imitated in the matter of multiple plots. I feel this way despite the fact that the divine Ariosto, through natural felicity and assiduous care and through his varied knowledge of things and his long apprenticeship to the outstanding writers (whereby he acquired a precise sense of the good and beautiful), reached a height of accomplishment in heroic poetry that no modern and few ancients have attained. I still think he should not be imitated in the matter of multiple plots; for such multiplicity will never be deemed praiseworthy, though it may well be possible to pardon it in a heroic poem by assigning the blame to the custom of the times or to a prince's or lady's request or to some other cause.

Neither passion nor recklessness nor chance moves me to say so; but certain arguments, whether true or verisimilar, have the power to sway or secure my mind in this conviction; for painting and the other imitative arts require that imitation of one thing be one. And philosophers, who always look for precision and perfection in things, expect unity of subject among the primary requisite conditions in their books; and when unity is missing, they deem the subject faulty. Finally, everybody judges unity necessary in tragedy and comedy. Why, then, must this unity be shunned and scorned in the epic poem when it is sought by philosophers, pursued by painters and sculptors, and retained by

118

comic writers and their fellows, the tragedians? If unity causes perfection in nature and multiplicity causes imperfection— wherefore Pythagoreans count the former among goods and the latter among evils and attribute the latter to matter and the former to form—why should unity not cause greater perfection than multiplicity in a heroic poem?

Further, suppose the plot is the poet's main purpose, as Aristotle affirmed and no one has yet denied.[26] If the plot is single, his purpose will be single; if there are many and diverse plots, there will be many and diverse purposes. However, since diverse purposes distract the mind and hinder labor, he who sets himself a single goal will work more effectively than the imitator of a multitude of actions. I add that multiple plots cause confusion, which could go on and on forever if art did not set and prescribe limits. The poet who treats one plot has reached his goal when that one plot is finished; he who weaves together more may interweave four or six or ten: he is no more obliged to one number than to another. Thus, he can have no sure sense at what point he had best stop.

Finally, the plot is the essential form of the poem, as no one doubts; so if the plots are distinct and independent of each other, it follows that there will be more poems than one. Then, since the so-called poem of many actions is not a single poem but many strung together, such poems are either complete or incomplete. If complete, they need the requisite length, having which, they become bulkier than the tomes of lawyers; if incomplete, better to write one single complete poem than many incomplete ones. I shall pass over the point that if these poems are, by nature, many and distinct—as appears from the multitude and distinctiveness of the plots—they are not merely confusing; rather, the mingling and intertwining of their parts, one with another, is monstrous, resembling that beast Dante describes in this tercet (and in the one that follows it):

Ellera abbarbicata mai non fue
ad arbor sì, come l'orribil fera
per l'altrui membra aviticchiò le sue.
(*Inferno* 25.58–60)

119

Ivy never clung so close to a tree as the horrible beast fastened his limbs to those of the other.

However, since I have said that the poem of many actions is many poems and, before that, have said that the *Innamorato* and the *Furioso* are a single poem, let no one think that I contradict myself. Here, I understand the word to mean exactly what it rightly and truly means; there, I used it as it is commonly used, that is, a single composition of actions—as we say, a single story.

Compelled, perhaps, by these reasons, or by others he perceived that do not occur to me, Aristotle decided that the plot of an epic should be single; and Horace accepted this as a good decision when he wrote, "Let the subject matter be simple and single."[27] Various critics, for various reasons, have taken issue with this decision; and they have excluded unity of plot from those heroic poems called romances—not merely because it is unnecessary (they say) but, indeed, because it is detrimental. But I do not want to report everything that they say on this subject because some of their points are extremely trivial and childish and entirely unworthy of responses. I will only present those arguments which confirm this opinion of theirs with the greatest semblance of truth; and these can be reduced altogether to the following four.

The romance (as they call the *Furioso* and other poems like it) is a poetic genre different from the epic and unknown to Aristotle. Therefore, it is not bound by the rules that Aristotle gave for the epic. And though Aristotle says that unity of plot is necessary in the epic, he still does not say that it is proper for this poetry of romances, which is of a kind unknown to him. They add a second argument, which goes like this. By nature, every language has certain special and native qualities that in no way compare to other idioms, as becomes clearly apparent to whoever scrupulously considers how many things have wondrous grace and energy in Greek that remain cold and dull in Latin and how many sound weak in Italian that have strength and power in Latin. However, among other qualities inherent in our Italian tongue, one is this—a capacity for a multitude of actions; and just as a multitude of actions would be unsuitable for writers of

DISCOURSES ON THE ART OF POETRY

Greek and Latin, so unity of plot does not suit writers of Italian. Beyond this, those poems are better which are approved by precedent, which has both authority and power over poetry, as over other matters. Horace bears witness to this where he says:

penes quem et ius et norma loquendi.[28]
(*Ars poetica* 72)

[Usage] in whose hands is the right and rule of speech.

But precedent more approves this type of poetry called romance, so it must be judged better. Finally, they conclude thus: that poem is a more perfect poem that better pursues the aim of poetry, which is much better and more easily pursued by romance than by epic, that is, by a multitude, rather than by a unity, of actions. Therefore, the romance must be preferred to the epic. And that romance better pursues this aim is so well known that it hardly here requires any proof, since delight is the aim of poetry and poems with more than a single plot give greater delight, as experience demonstrates.

These are the foundations that support the opinion of those who deem a multitude of actions appropriate in romances. Indeed, they are firm and sure, but not so much so that the devices of reason cannot overcome them—if only reason forms the opposition, as I like to think it does. Confident in this argument, my frail intellect does not hesitate to counter them.

We come to the first basic point, which says that the romance is a genre distinct from the epic and unknown to Aristotle; therefore, it does not have to submit to those rules to which he bound the epic. If the romance is a genre distinct from the epic, it is clear that it is distinct through some essential difference, because incidental differences cannot cause a generic divergence. However, since we find no essential[29] difference between the epic and the romance, it clearly follows that there is no generic distinction between them. And it can readily be made clear to anyone that there is no essential difference between them. In poetry, there are only three essential differences, from which arise, as from various sources, various and distinct types

121

of poems. They are, as we said in the preceding discourse, a difference in the things imitated, a difference in the manner of imitation, and a difference in the means of imitation. Through these differences alone do epic poets, comic poets, tragic poets, and rhapsodists differ;[30] and from these differences would arise the generic divergence between epic and romance, if there were any. But romance and epic imitate the same actions, they imitate in the same manner, and they imitate with the same means; they are, therefore, the same genre.

Epic and romance imitate the same actions, the illustrious; nor is that similarity—imitating the illustrious in general—the only similarity between tragic and epic poets; there is, further, the closer and more particular likeness of imitating the same kind of illustriousness. I am not talking about the illustrious based on the grandeur of horrible and pathetic deeds but about the illustrious based upon the noble and magnanimous actions of heroes. I am not talking about that illustrious which deals with persons midway between vice and virtue but about that illustrious which deals with persons of the highest rank and excellence. This similarity in imitating the same kind of illustriousness clearly appears in our romances and in the epics of the Greeks and Romans. Romance and epic imitate in the same manner: the person of the poet appears in both; both tell stories, they do not reenact them; nor are they intended for the stage and the performance of actors, as are comedy and tragedy. They imitate by the same means: both employ plain verse without making use of rhythm and harmony, which belong to the tragic and the comic poet.

Thus, from the similarity of the actions imitated and of the means and manner of imitation, we conclude that what we call epic and what we call romance belong to the same genre of poetry. Whence this name *romance* derives there are various opinions, which we need not recount now. It is not inappropriate, however, to find classed in the same genre some poems that differ through incidental differences and that are called by different names. So it happens with comedies that some are called *stataria*, or stationary, and others [are called] . . . , that some take their name from the *sagum*, or mantle, and others take it

122

from the toga; but all abide by the precepts and rules essential to comedy, like this one about unity.[31] So if epic and romance are the same genre of poetry, they must be bound by the same rules, especially when we are talking about those rules which are absolutely necessary not only in any heroic poem but in any poem whatever. Such is unity of plot, which Aristotle requires in any type of poem, as well in the heroic as in the tragic or the comic. Thus, even if what is said were true—that romance is not epic poetry—it would not therefore follow that in Aristotle's view it did not need unity of plot.

That this is so appears to me amply proven because those who would prove that romance is a different genre from epic must show that Aristotle is mistaken and inadequate when making distinctions. And whoever well considers those differences from which proceeds a generic difference between epic and romance will see that they are incidental, just as it is incidental, when a man exercises, whether he does so by riding or wrestling or fencing. Such is the distinction that the theme of a romance is invented and that of an epic derives from history. For if this were a generic difference, those poems in which this difference occurs must needs differ generically. Thus, Agathon's *Flower* and Sophocles' *Oedipus* would differ generically, and likewise those tragedies whose theme is invented would differ generically from those which take theirs from history. Also, according to this reasoning, the same rules would not bind a tragedy with an invented theme as bind a tragedy with a historical theme. There-fore, unity of plot would be unnecessary in it, and arousing terror and pity would not be its aim. But without any doubt this is inappropriate, and it would be inappropriate even if the inven-tion or the historical truth of a theme were a generic difference.

The other differences that they point out have the same worth and can be disproved by the same principles from the same reasoning. And since many have believed that romance is a poetic genre unknown to Aristotle, I am unwilling to keep silence: there is surely no poetic genre today in use, nor was there such in ancient times, nor will such arise in a long cycle of centuries, that Aristotle did not fathom. And with the same intellectual acumen, he arranged under ten headings everything that God and nature enclose in this great cosmos; and likewise, by reducing so many different syllogisms to a few small forms, he composed them into a complete brief art.[32] That art, unknown to ancient philosophers unless they practiced it instinctively, recognized its first principles and final perfection through him alone. Aristotle saw that the nature of poetry was nothing other than imitation. Consequently, he saw that poetry's generic differences could not otherwise arise than through some difference in imitation and that such variation could occur only in three ways: in the things imitated, in the manner of imitation, or in the means of imitation. Thus, he saw how many essential differences there could be in poetry and, having seen these differences, he saw in consequence how many poetic genres there could be; for when those differences that make up the genres are determined, the genres themselves must be determined, and they are only as many as the ways in which those differences can be brought together or combined.

The second argument was that each language has some particular properties and that a multitude of actions is appropriate for Tuscan poems, as is unity for Latin and Greek poems. I do not deny that each language has some qualities peculiar to itself, since we do see some expressions so peculiar to one language that they cannot be effectively translated into another. The Greek language is well suited to express every minute detail; Latin is ill suited to such expression but much more capable of grandeur and majesty; and although our Tuscan language does not fill our ears with a comparable sound when describing warfare, it nonetheless beguiles us with greater sweetness when handling amorous feelings. Thus, what is peculiar to a language may be phrasing and locution, which do not pertain to our concern, since we are speaking of actions, not words.

Or, we may call those subjects peculiar to a language which it handles better than another, as war in Latin and love in Tuscan. It is clear, however, that if Tuscan is suited to express many amorous incidents, it is equally suited to express one; and if Latin best handles one military affair, it can, as well, handle many. So, for myself, I cannot understand why unity of action is peculiar to Latin poems and a multitude of actions is peculiar to vernacular

124

poems. Perhaps there is no explanation. If someone should ask me why military subjects are considered better-suited for Latin and amorous subjects for Tuscan, I would answer this way: Latin is said to be better suited to the uproar of armies and to warfare because of its many consonants and the length of its hexameter line, and Tuscan is better-adapted to the pleasure of amorous feelings because of its vowels and the harmony of its rhymes. These subjects, however, are not so peculiar to these languages that an excellent poet cannot give appropriate words to warfare in Tuscan and to love in Latin. I say, then, in conclusion: even though it is quite true that each language has its own peculiarities, it is nonetheless completely unreasonable to maintain that a multitude of actions is peculiar to vernacular poems and unity of action is peculiar to poems in Latin and Greek.

It is no more difficult to answer the argument that says those poems are superior that custom gives more approval to and, therefore, that romance is superior to epic because custom approves of it more. Since I want to counter this argument, it is best to base my reasoning on a higher principle in order to achieve greater clarity and understanding of the truth.

There are some things that are neither good nor evil by nature, but that depend on custom; and they are good or evil as custom determines them. Dress is such a thing; it is praiseworthy inasmuch as fashion allows. Speech is the same; so this was an apt response: "Live the way the ancients lived and speak the way we speak today."[33] Thus, it happens that many words that were once select and exotic have now become trite, common, base, and vulgar. On the other hand many once avoided as barbaric and frightful are now accepted as lovely and civilized. Many words grow old, many die; many others are born and will be born, as it pleases custom, which controls them with free and full sway. Horace admirably expresses this change in words when he compares them to the leaves:

Ut silvae foliis pronos mutantur in annos,
prima cadunt, ita verborum vetus interit aetas,
et iuvenum ritu florent modo nata vigentque.
(*Ars poetica* 60–62)

125

As the woods change their leaves with each year's decline, and the oldest drop off first: so with words, the old race dies and the new-born bloom and thrive like youths.

And he adds:

Multa renascentur quae iam cecidere, cadentque
quae nunc sunt in honore vocabula, si volet usus
quem penes arbitrium est et ius et norma loquendi.
(Ars poetica 70–72)

Many terms that have fallen out of use shall be born again, and those now esteemed shall fall, if usage wills it so—in whose hands is the right and rule and standard of speech.

For this reason the peripatetics concluded, contrary to what some philosophers believed, that words are not works of nature, nor do they by nature signify one thing more than another. If they were such, they would not depend on custom. They are, however, human products denoting nothing in themselves; and therefore, they can signify now this idea and now that one, as we please. Since no beauty or ugliness is peculiar or native to them, they appear beautiful or ugly as custom decides; and custom being changeable in the extreme, all things that depend on it are necessarily changeable. In sum, not only are dress and speech this way, but so are all those things called, in common usage, "customs." As their name shows, fashion assigns them praise or blame. Many of those objections made about the decorum of Homer's characters—a decorum some say he was hardly aware of—give way in this light.

We find some other things that are the way they are by their nature; that is, they are good or evil in themselves, and custom has no rule or authority over them. Vice and virtue are of this kind: vice in itself is wicked, virtue in itself is honorable, and virtuous and vicious deeds in themselves are praiseworthy and blameworthy. Whatever is this way in itself will always be this way, even though the world and customs change. If he once deserved praise who refused the gold of the Samnites or who "bound himself while alive and set free his father who was

126

dead," these actions will never warrant censure through the passage of time.[34] Works of nature are equally of this sort, so what was once excellent will always be excellent despite the uncertainty of custom. Nature is most certain in her workings and always advances in a sure and steady manner (even though she seems to change through some material defect or instability). Guided by an unerring light, she always attends to the good and the perfect; and since the good and the perfect are always the same, her way of working must always be the same. Beauty is a work of nature that consists in a certain proportion of parts, as well as appropriate size and lovely grace of coloring.[35] These conditions, which were at one time beautiful in themselves, will always be beautiful; and custom cannot make them seem otherwise. So, by contrast, custom cannot make pointed heads and goitres beautiful among those nations where such qualities appear in the majority of men.

If works of nature are this way in themselves, works of art, which imitate nature, must also be this way in themselves. To pause at the examples given, if the proportion of the parts is beautiful in itself, this same thing will be beautiful in itself when the painter or sculptor imitates it; and if the natural object be praiseworthy, the artificial object based on it will be praiseworthy. Thus, it happens that those statues of Praxiteles or Phidias which have survived the cruelty of time appear as beautiful to men of today as they used to appear to the ancients. Neither the passage of so many centuries nor the change of so many customs has been able to diminish anything of their dignity.

Having made this distinction, I can easily respond to the argument that says those poems are most excellent which custom gives most approval to. Every poem is composed of words and things. As for words, granted (since it does not pertain to my point) those are the best that custom recommends more than others, since in themselves they are neither beautiful nor ugly—rather, usage makes them seem whatever they seem. Thus, words that were prized by King Enzo[36] and by other ancient writers sound somewhat unpleasant to our ears. Things that depend on custom (for example, ways of fighting, methods of travel, rites of sacrifice and dining, the decorum and dignity

127

of persons)—these things, I say, must accommodate the customs that now exist and hold sway. Thus, the dignity of our times would not allow a king's daughter, together with her maiden companions, to go wash clothes in a river; yet it was suitable for Homer's Nausicaa in those times.[37] Likewise, it would be unsuitable to substitute fighting from chariots for jousting—and many similar things that I shall skip over for brevity's sake. So Trissino seemed ill-advised when he imitated those things in Homer which the change in customs had rendered less commendable.

But those things which are based immediately upon nature and are good and commendable in themselves have no concern with convention, and the tyranny of custom affects them not at all. Such is unity of plot, which by its very nature brings goodness and perfection to a poem, just as in every past and future epoch it has brought and will bring them. Such are customs—not those we call fashion but those which have fixed their roots in nature—of which Horace speaks in these lines:

> Reddere qui voces iam scit puer et pede certo
> signat humum, gestit paribus colludere et iram
> colligit et ponit temere: mutatur in horas.
> (Ars poetica 158–60)

> The child, who by now can talk in words and prints firm steps upon the ground, enjoys playing with his mates; he is swift to anger and to be appeased; he changes every hour.

Aristotle spends almost all of the second book of his *Rhetoric* on the appropriateness of such customs and human behavior. And regarding this human behavior of the young and the old, the rich, the powerful, the poor, and the ignoble, what is appropriate in one epoch is appropriate in any epoch. If this were not so, Aristotle would not have discussed it, since he professes to discuss only those things which concern art. Since art is sure and fixed, it cannot include in its rules those things which are unsure and changeable because of the instability of custom. Likewise, he would not have discussed unity of plot if he had not decided that this quality was necessary in any epoch. However, those

128

who wish to base a new art on new customs destroy the nature of art and show they do not understand the nature of custom.

Without this distinction, Signor Scipione, there is no response to those who ask whether they ought to imitate the epics of ancient authors or the poems of modern romancers, because we ought to conform to the ancients in some matters and to the moderns in others. Common people misunderstand, because they usually study the incidentals, and not the essentials, of things. When they observe the slight appropriateness of customs and the limited charm of inventions in poems with a single plot, they believe unity of plot deserves the blame. Some learned people who misunderstand this same distinction are induced to repudiate the charm of adventures and chivalry in romances, as well as the decorum of modern customs, and to defend, along with unity of plot in the ancients, other less worthy qualities. If this distinction is well understood and well employed, ordinary men will observe the precepts of art as readily as intellectuals. On the one hand, they will avail themselves of the decorum of customs, which, along with the charm of invention, makes romances so pleasing; on the other, they will avail themselves of the gravity and verisimilitude that appear in the poems of Homer and Virgil, along with unity of plot.

The final argument remains. It says that since delight is the aim of poetry, those poems are most excellent which best achieve this aim and that the romance achieves this better than the epic, as experience shows. I concede that which I think true and which many would deny, that is, that the aim of poetry is delight. Likewise, I concede what experience shows, that is, that the *Furioso* gives people of our time greater delight than the *Italia liberata* or even than the *Iliad* or the *Odyssey*. I deny, however, that a multitude of actions can give more delight than a single action; and this is essential to my point and matters absolutely—for even though the *Furioso*, which has many plots, gives more delight than the *Italia liberata* or even the poems of Homer, which have a single plot, this does not depend on unity or multiplicity but, rather, on two causes that do not pertain at all to my point. First, love, chivalry, adventure, and enchantment occur in the *Furioso*—all of them inventions lovelier and more appealing

129

than those of Trissino. And such inventions are not more confined to multiplicity than to unity but can as well be found in one as in the other. Second, the *Furioso* proves itself far superior in appropriateness of customs and in the decorum of the characters. Since these reasons are incidental to multiplicity and unity of plot and not so suited to the former as to be ill-suited to the latter, we need not conclude that multiplicity delights more than unity. Since humanity includes natures quite unlike one another, it is not necessarily pleased by one and the same thing all the time; rather, through diversity, now one part, now another, finds satisfaction. Therefore, we can conceive a single argument more appropriate than the others aforementioned—and that is variety.

Variety is, by nature, extremely delightful; and greater variety appears in multiplicity, than in unity, of plot. Nor do I deny that variety gives pleasure; to deny that would contradict the facts of our feelings, since we perceive that things unpleasant in themselves become pleasant through variation and the sight of deserts and the frightful ruggedness of the Alps please us after the charm of lakes and gardens. I maintain that variety warrants praise until it becomes confusing and that up to this point unity of plot is as capable of variety as is multiplicity. If such variety does not appear in a poem of a single action, we should deem it due rather to the artist's lack of skill than to a defect of the art, though such artists frequently ascribe their mistakes to the art to excuse their own inadequacy.

Perhaps this variety was not so necessary in Virgil's and Homer's times, since the tastes of men of that epoch were not so jaded. Therefore, they did not concern themselves so much about it, though greater variety appears in Virgil than in Homer. In our times it is especially necessary; and Trissino, therefore, needed to season his poem with the spice of this variety so that delicate tastes would not shun it. If he did not try to use variety in his poem, he may not have recognized the need for it, or he may have despaired of the possibility of using it. For myself, I deem variety in a heroic poem both necessary and possible to attain.

In this marvelous domain of God that we call the world we

130

see the sky sprinkled and adorned with so great a variety of
stars; and, descending from realm to realm, we see the air and
ocean full of birds and fish, and the earth a hospice to so many
animals both wild and tame, and on earth streams and fountains
and lakes and meadows and fields and forests and mountains,
and here fruits and flowers, there ice and snow, here dwellings
and farmlands, there wastelands and emptiness. Nonetheless,
the earth, which encloses so many and diverse things in its
bosom, is one; and its form and essence are one; and one, the
knot by which it joins and binds its parts in discordant concord.
While it lacks nothing, nothing in it is excessive and unnecessary. Just so, I think an excellent poet—who is called divine for
no other reason except that by working like the supreme Artificer he comes to share in his divinity—can shape a poem in
which, as in a little world, we read of mustering armies, land
and sea battles, conquests of cities, skirmishes and duels, jousts,
drought and starvation, tempests, fires, prodigies; and we find
heavenly and hellish assemblies and see sedition, discord, wanderings, adventures, enchantments, cruelty, boldness, courtesy,
kindness, and love—sometimes happy, sometimes sad, sometimes joyous, sometimes pitiful. And still, the poem which contains such a variety of matter is one; its form and its plot are
one; and all these things are brought together in such a way that
one thing shows consideration for another, one thing corresponds to another, and through either necessity or verisimilitude one thing depends on another in such a way that by remov-
ing a single part or by changing its place, we destroy the whole.

Such unity will warrant greater praise, the greater the challenge it poses for itself, since it is very easy and requires no
effort to produce a great variety of incidents in many separate
actions; but to discover similar variety in one single action—*hoc
opus, hic labor est*.[38] The former variety, which arises of its own
accord from the multitude of plots, in no way reveals the poet's
art and genius; and the untaught can manage it as well as the
learned. The latter variety depends entirely on the poet's art
and occurs through his art alone, like its natural product; and no
middling talent can attain such variety. All in all, the former
variety delights less and less as it becomes more confused and

131

unintelligible; the latter is not merely clearer and more to the point through the order and fit of its parts, it provides greater novelty and wonder, as well. The plot and the form, then, should be one in those poems that deal with the battles and loves of heroes and knights-errant and are commonly called heroic poems, as well as in every other kind of poem. But the form is called one in several senses. We call one the form of elements, that is the simplest—simple in power and simple in function; likewise, we call one the mixed and composite form of plants and animals, which results from gathering together the forms of elements and shaping and changing them and sharing among them the power and quality of each one. Similarly, we find in poetry some simple forms and some composite forms. The plots are simple in those tragedies which contain no recognition and no change of fortune from happy to sad or vice versa; and they are composite in those which contain recognition and reversal of fortune.[39] Epic plots are composite not only in this way but in yet another, which entails greater mixture.

To understand these terms better and to clarify the subject further, I shall develop this part more amply. If we believe Aristotle, the plot is the sequence and composition of the things imitated. This is the primary qualitative part of the poem, and it has some qualitative parts of its own, as well. These are three: peripeteia, which we can call change of fortune; *anagnorisis*, which we can call recognition; and perturbation, which we can still call by this name in Tuscan.[40] The plot contains change of fortune when some shift from happiness to misery appears in it, as with Oedipus, or from misery to happiness, as with Electra. Recognition, as the name itself indicates, means a passage from ignorance to awareness. It may be either simple, like Ulysses', or reciprocal, like that between Iphigenia and Orestes; and this passage may cause either grief or happiness. Perturbation is a grievous and sorrowful action, like deaths and tortures and wounds and similar things that stir cries and laments from the persons involved. The last book of the *Iliad* exemplifies this, where Hector's death is bewailed and sorrowed over by Priam and Hecuba and Andromache with a lengthy and tearful lament.

With this matter standing thus, those plots are simple which lack change of fortune and recognition and, proceeding directly, reach their end without any variation. Those plots are double which contain change of fortune and recognition or, at least, the first of these. Likewise, those are called pathetic or sentimental which contain perturbation, which was established as the third aspect of the plot. And contrariwise, those which lack perturbation and incline more toward the show of customs and give delight more through instruction than emotion are called moral (or social). So there are four kinds of plots, or ways of naming them: simple, composite, pathetic, and moral.[41] The *Iliad* is simple and pathetic, the *Odyssey*, composite and moral.[42] Unity, however, is required in all these kinds, though unity of the simple plot is simple unity and unity of the composite plot is composite unity. Moreover, the plot of a poem can be considered composite in another sense. Though it does not contain recognition or change of fortune, we call it composite when it contains in itself things of diverse natures (like wars and loves and enchantments and adventures and events either happy or sad) that sometimes involve terror and pity, sometimes beauty and joy. A mixture results from these diverse natures, but a mixture much different from the first; and we can find among these plots some that are still simple—that is, they contain neither change of fortune nor recognition.

Aristotle showed an understanding of this second kind of mixture when, discussing whether tragedy or epic has greater dignity, he stated that tragic plots are much simpler than those of epics. That a single epic can supply subjects for many tragedies supports the truth of his insight. In tragedy, this second kind of mixture deserves criticism just as the other kind, which arises from reversal and from recognition, deserves praise; for although tragedy greatly favors sudden and unexpected change of circumstance, it wants these circumstances simple and uniform, and it avoids variety of episodes. That same mixture that warrants blame in tragedy is most praiseworthy in epic, I think, and much more necessary than that mixture which derives from recognition and change of fortune. Therefore, the epic poet seeks a multitude and variety of episodes. And if Aristotle condemns episodic plots, either he condemns them in tragedy alone or he does not consider plots that contain many and various episodes as episodic plots. Rather, he considers as such those plots whose episodes are introduced despite verisimilitude and are ill connected to the plot and are in themselves disjointed. Episodes of this sort are, in sum, vain and self-indulgent and of no effect toward the main aim of the plot; for a variety of episodes deserves praise inasmuch as it does not undermine the unity of the plot or cause confusion in it. I am speaking of that unity which is composite, not that which is simple and uniform and little-suited to the heroic poem.

But perhaps it is in order, and the subject requires, that in the following discourse, there should be some discussion of the art by which the poet introduces into the unified plot this variety, which is so pleasing and so much desired by those whose ears have grown accustomed to the adventurous tales of our romancers.[43]

Discourse 3

Since I intend to discuss diction, I will consequently discuss style.[44] Since diction is no more than the joining together of words and words are no more than images and imitators of ideas (whose natures words reflect), I must discuss style, which is no more than the composite that results from ideas and words.

There are three types of style: the magnificent or sublime, the middle, and the low. The first of these suits the heroic poem for two reasons: first, because the lofty things that the epic chooses to treat must be dealt with in the highest style; second, because every part works toward the same end that the whole works toward. Since style is part of the epic, it works toward the same end as the epic, which is wonder; and wonder arises only from sublime and magnificent things.

Therefore, magnificence suits the epic as its own proper style. I say its own proper style because this style predominates even though the others must be used depending on the events

134

and the subjects, as appears most clearly in Virgil—just as earth predominates in our bodies, which are composed, nonetheless, of all four elements. We must call Trissino's style low because the low prevails in it; and, for the same reason, we call Ariosto's the middle style. It is worth noting that just as each virtue has some vice kindred to it, which resembles it and is often called by the virtue's name, likewise each kind of style has its own corresponding defect, which the careless often blunder into. Magnificence becomes swollen, the middle style becomes dry and lifeless, and the low, base and vulgar. The magnificent, the middle, and the low are not the same in heroic poems as they are in other poems; rather, just as other poems differ in genre from the heroic, the styles likewise differ from genre to genre. Therefore, the low style is sometimes appropriate in a heroic poem; however, the low style appropriate in comedy is inappropriate in an heroic poem, as Ariosto shows when he writes:

> Ch'a dire il vero, egli ci avea la gola;
> . . . .
> e riputata avria cortesia sciocca,
> per darla altrui, levarsela di bocca,[45]
>   (*Orlando furioso* 10.10.5, 7–8)

For, to tell the truth, he had an appetite for her himself, . . . and he would have deemed it foolish courtesy to take her out of his own mouth to give her to another.

And in these other verses:

> E dicea il ver; ch'era viltade espressa
> conveniente ad uom fatto di stucco,
> . . . .
> che tutta via stesse a parlar con essa,
> tende l'ale basse come il cucco.[46]
>   (*Orlando furioso* 25.31.1–2, 5–6)

And she spoke the truth, for it was obvious baseness befitting a man made of plaster who—finding himself with such a lovely, nectar-sweet woman—nevertheless kept on talking with her, trailing his wings like the cuckoo bird.

135

To tell the truth, the language of the first is too common, and that of the second tends toward the vulgarity of comedy because it presents something dishonorable, which is always unsuited to the heroic poem. Similarly, these lines:

> E fe' raccorre al suo destrier le penne,
> ma non a tal che più l'avea distese.
> Del destrier sceso, a pena si ritenne
> di salir altri.
> > (*Orlando furioso* 10.114.3–6)

> And he made his flying charger fold his wings but not that thing that made them spread the wider. He dismounted from the steed but scarcely restrained himself from mounting another.

And although the lyric and the epic have more in common, Ariosto inclines too much toward the middle style of the lyric in these lines:

> La virginella è simile alla rosa, etc.
> > (*Orlando furioso* 1.42.1)

> The young virgin is like the rose, etc.

·The heroic style lies midway between the plainspoken seriousness of tragedy and the intricate loveliness of the lyric, and it surpasses both in the majesty of its wonderful stateliness; however, its stateliness is less ornate than the lyric and less restrained than tragedy. Nonetheless, it is not inappropriate for an epic poet to depart from the terms of his genre's illustrious magnificence. As I shall clarify in what follows, he sometimes inclines toward tragic simplicity and sometimes toward lyric excess, though more rarely toward the latter and more often toward the former.

Though tragedy can well accommodate illustrious events and royal persons, its style needs to be more restrained and less magnificent than that of epic for two reasons. First, it deals with subjects that are much more emotional than those of the epic; and emotion requires purity and simplicity of expression and restrained diction, because it is likely that a person would speak in this way when full of anguish or fear or pity or other similar emotions. Besides, the bright lights and ornaments of style not only dim feeling, they impair and smother it. Second, in tragedy the poet never speaks in his own voice, but those who are introduced as agents and actors do the speaking; and it is necessary to give these a way of speaking that resembles ordinary speech so that the imitation will be more verisimilar. However, when the poet speaks in his own person, he is allowed to think and speak as though with a different mind and a different tongue and much beyond ordinary usage, because we believe him inspired and rapt with divine *furor*.

The lyric style, then, although not so magnificent as epic, must be much more intricate and ornate; and, as the rhetoricians affirm, the intricate manner of speech belongs to the middle style. Lyric style must be intricate both because the poet often appears in his own person and because lyric chooses to treat subjects that are less active and that would remain base and abject if unadorned. Therefore, if a moral subject were by chance given lyric treatment, it would happily settle for less ornamentation.

Since it is clear why the lyric style is intricate and why the tragic style is pure and simple, the epic poet will see why he must approach the restraint and simplicity of tragedy when dealing with a pathetic or moral subject; however, when speaking in his own person or dealing with an inactive subject, he must come near to lyric beauty. But he must do neither the former nor the latter to the extent that he totally abandons his own proper grandeur and magnificence. He must make use of this variety of styles but not so that he changes styles without a change in subject, for that would be a most serious imperfection.

How To Attain This Magnificent Style and How To Develop the Middle and Low Styles

Magnificence can arise from ideas, from words, and from combinations of words.[47] Style derives from these three sources, as do those three types of style which we named. Ideas are no more than images of things. Unlike things, these images have no real or solid substance in themselves; but they have a certain imperfect being in our minds, and thence they are shaped and formed by the imagination. The magnificence of ideas comes from dealing with grand themes like God, the world, heroes, land and sea battles, and the like.[48] To express such grandeur, those figures of speech are suitable that make themes and their contexts appear grand, like amplification or hyperbole, which exalt a theme beyond the truth of the matter;[49] or like understatement, which leaves much to the imagination by bringing up a subject and then falling silent about it; or like personification, which gives authority and reverence to a theme by creating characters with authority and reverence;[50] or like other similar figures that do not come easily to the minds of ordinary men and are apt to induce wonder—for the proper sphere of the poet of the magnificent style is stirring and transporting minds, just as the poet of the low style instructs and the poet of the middle style delights, even though the reader may find some delight in being transported or instructed. Diction will be sublime if the words are not ordinary but exotic and far from everyday speech.[51]

Words are either simple or compound: those are simple which are not composed of meaningful elements; those are compound which are composed of two meaningful elements or of one element with meaning and another without.[52] These words are either native or foreign, metaphorical, decorative, made up, lengthened or contracted, or modified. Those are native which apply to something authoritatively and that are commonly used by all the inhabitants of a country, and those are foreign which are in use in another nation. The same word can be both native and foreign with respect to different nations: *chero* is native to Spaniards, foreign to us. Metaphor is the imposition of other terms, and this occurs in four ways: from genus to species, from species to genus, from species to species, or by means of analogy.[53] We use the genus for the species when we call a horse a beast, and the species for the genus if we say "that man famous for a thousand deeds" instead of using a general name. We use one species for another when we say that a horse flies. We employ analogy in this way: there is the same relation between

138

daytime and sunset as there is between life and death. Thus, we can say that sunset is "the death of the day," as does Dante:

Che parea il giorno pianger che si more.[54]
(*Purgatorio* 8.6)

It [the bell] seems to cry for the day which is dying.

And we can say that death is "the sunset of life":

La vita in su 'l mattin giunse a l'occaso.[55]

In its morning, his life attained its sunset.

Those words are made up which are created by the poet and have never been used before, like *taratantara*[56], which both signifies and imitates the blowing of a trumpet. Those words are lengthened in which either a short vowel becomes long, as in *simile*, or to which a syllable has been added, as in *adiviene*. Those are contracted which have undergone the opposite changes. Those are modified in which some letter has been altered, as in *despitto* instead of *dispetto*.

The sublime and the exotic in diction derive from foreign words and from metaphors and from all those words that are not entirely familiar.[57] But obscurity also arises from these same sources, and it is just as much to be avoided in a heroic poem as clarity—even more than magnificence—is to be sought. Judiciousness is needed, however, in combining foreign words with native ones so that they result in an entirely clear and entirely sublime composition that is in no way obscure or lowly. Therefore, metaphors must be chosen that have the closest kinship with common speech; and the same holds true for foreign and ancient and other such words, and these should be combined with native words that have nothing plebeian about them. Our language does not allow the compounding of words, and we should also, as much as possible, avoid lengthening and contracting them. With regard to metaphor, take heed to avoid those figures of speech which have been debased through common usage. Further, comparisons should not liken larger things

139

to smaller ones, like thunder to a trumpet blast, but smaller ones to larger, like trumpeting to a roll of thunder; for the latter figure wonderfully elevates what the former lowers and debases.[58]

Such heed should also be taken with images or (let us say) with similes, which derive from metaphors with the addition of one of the following particles: *like*, *as*, and others.[59] The image becomes a comparison when it is carried to greater length and has more parts; and rhetoricians advise that when metaphors appear strained to us, we should turn them into similes. But certainly we should praise an epic poet's daring in such metaphors so long as they do not exceed the limit.

Foreign words should be drawn from languages kindred to our own, like Provençal, French, and Spanish. I will add Latin to these languages, provided that we inflect its words with Tuscan endings. Specific attributes of the lyric style are appropriate for the epic poet. Though the orator makes no use of them because they are unnecessary to his art, they are a source of great magnificence for the poet, and he employs them as a great ornament.

The composition of sentences is the third aspect of style, and it will have magnificence if the periods and their component parts are long.[60] For this reason, the stanza can better sustain the heroic style than the tercet. Magnificence is increased by asperity, which derives from the assonance of vowels, from enjambment, from a fullness of consonants in the rhymes, from intensifying the rhythm at the end of the verse, or from words that are keenly felt through vigorous accentuation or alliteration. Likewise, the frequency of the connectives enhances magnificence, for they strengthen the discourse like sinews. Sometimes unusual positioning of the verb, if done rarely, ennobles speech.

To avoid the vice of an inflated style, the poet of magnificence eschews certain minute refinements, such as making phrases correspond with phrases, verbs with verbs, and nouns with nouns; and this applies not only to rhythm but also to meaning.[61] Avoid antitheses like

140

Tu veloce fanciullo, io vecchio e tardo.[62]
(Bembo, "Se tutti i miei prim'anni," verse 11)

You swift and young, I old and slow.

For all of these figures, which betray affectation, suit the middle
style; and because they delight us a great deal, they do not move
us at all.

Magnificence of style derives from the aforementioned
sources; and the same sources (or others like them), when they
are used at the wrong time, cause an inflated style, which is the
vice akin to magnificence. The inflated style comes from the
ideas if they exceed the truth by too great a distance, as when, for
example, the boulder hurled by the Cyclops is said to have goats
grazing on it while it travels through the air.[63] The inflated style
comes from words when they are too exotic or too ancient, or
when epithets are unbecoming, or when metaphors are too
strained and too daring.[64] Tumidity arises from the composition
of sentences if the discourse is not merely rhythmical but exces-
sively so, as in many passages of Boccaccio's prose. Inflation of
style is like vainglory, which exults in virtues that it does not
possess and employs those that it does at the wrong moment.[65]
Therefore, a style that is magnificent when applied to matters of
importance is called inflated when it is applied to affairs of no
consequence. It is not true that the power of eloquence, either in
oratory or in poetry, consists in magnificent speech about inconse-
quential matters; even though Virgil described the republic of the
bees in a magnificent manner, he did so only as a joke; for in
serious affairs, one always aims to have the words and the composition of the sentences in keeping with the ideas.[66]

The low style derives from opposite sources. First, the ideas
are low when they are exactly such as ordinarily arise in people's
minds; and they are not apt to induce wonder, but they are
instead suited for teaching.[67] The diction is low when the words
are native and not exotic, novel, or foreign; and when it contains few figures of speech, and they are not daring, as befits the
magnificent style; and when it contains few epithets and such as

141

are necessary, rather than ornamental. The composition of the sentences is low when the periods and their parts are brief, when the discourse has few connectives and proceeds easily in accordance with common usage and without transposing nouns or verbs, when the verses are unbroken, and when the line endings are not too carefully chosen. Baseness is the vice akin to this style, and this occurs in the ideas when they are too vile and vulgar and they contain obscenity and filth. The diction is base when the words are rustic and vulgar. The composition of the sentences is base whenever it lacks rhythm altogether and the verse is totally slack, as:

> Poi vide Cleopatrà lussuriosa.[68]
> (*Inferno* 5.63)

Then I saw the lustful Cleopatra.

The middle style is situated between the magnificent and the low and partakes of both one and the other.[69] This style does not derive from mixing the magnificent and the low so that they are jumbled together but either from moderating the magnificent or exalting the low. In this form ideas and diction surpass the common usage of everyone; however, they do not carry as much weight and strength as the magnificent style requires. The quality by which the middle style particularly surpasses the ordinary manner of speaking is the loveliness in the precise and intricate ornaments of ideas and diction and in the sweetness and grace of composition. All such figures, which reveal precise and diligent effort and which neither the magnificent poet would deign, nor the low poet dare, to employ are put to work by the poet of the middle style. He may then run into that vice which is akin to a laudable middle style if he promotes surfeit and annoyance by the affectation that frequent use of such ornaments may entail.[70] The middle style does not have as much power to move people's minds as the magnificent does, nor is it so convincing about what it narrates; but it gives more delight with its graceful and temperate manner.

Given that style is the means by which the poet imitates those

142

things which he proposes to imitate, it must have clarity, which sets things before the eyes so that one seems not to hear them but to see them.[71] And this strength is all the more necessary in an epic poem than in a tragedy inasmuch as the former lacks the support of both actors and the stage. This virtue derives from a diligent precision in describing things in detail, for which, however, our language is ill-suited. Dante, nonetheless, seems to outdo himself in this regard and is perhaps worthy of comparison with Homer, who is foremost as far as language is concerned. We read in the *Purgatorio*:

> Come le pecorelle escon del chiuso
> ad una, a due, a tre, e l'altre stanno
> timidette atterrando l'occhio e 'l muso;
>   e ciò che fa la prima, e l'altre fanno,
> addossandosi a lei, s'ella s'arresta,
> semplici e quete, e lo perchè non sanno. . . .
> (Purgatorio 3.79–84)

As the sheep come out of the folds by ones, by twos, by threes, and the others stand by, fearful, turning their eye and muzzle to the ground; and whatever the first one does, the others do, simple and quiet, bumping into her if she stops; and they do not know why. . . .

This advantage also occurs when a speaker is given appropriate gestures:[72]

> Mi guardò un poco, e poi, quasi sdegnoso . . . . [73]
> (Dante, Inferno 10.41)

He eyed me a little, and then, almost with contempt . . . .

Such precise narration is required in emotional scenes because it is the principle means of arousing feelings, and the whole speech of Count Ugolino in the *Inferno* exemplifies this point.[74] This advantage also occurs if, when some effect is described, the circumstances that accompany it are also shown—as when, describing a ship's course, one says that the broken waves murmur around it. Figures of speech that represent things in action use this kind of expression, especially when they give life to inanimate objects:

insin che 'l ramo
vede alla terra tutte le sue spoglie.
(Dante, *Inferno* 3.113–14)

until the bough sees all its foliage on the ground.

Similarly, in Ariosto:

In tanto fugge e si dilegua il lito.[75]

The shore flees and disappears.

Likewise, we say "the avenging sword" and the sword "thirsty for blood" or "impious," "cruel," "rash," and so on. Clarity often derives from those words which are natural for what one wants to express.

Dante asserted that style does not arise from the idea but from the form of expression, and he thoroughly believed that this was the case. Therefore, he thought that the sonnet must not express important matters in the magnificent style but rather in the low, which is the composition and the quality of the sonnet, since the sonnet form is not appropriate for the magnificent style.[76] On the other hand, ideas are the end, and consequently the form, of the words and of the expressions. But the form should not be arranged to suit the material, nor should it depend upon the material—rather, just the opposite. Thus, the ideas should not depend on the words; rather, the truth is altogether otherwise: the words should be subject to the ideas and be ruled by them. The first proposition is proved because nature gave us speech for no other reason than to express the thoughts of our minds to others; and the second proposition is all too clear. There is a second argument. The images should be like the thing imagined or imitated; but according to Aristotle, words are images and imitators of ideas.[77] Therefore, the words must follow the nature of the ideas. The first proposition is very clear, because it would be extremely inappropriate to make a

144

statue of Venus that did not embody the grace and comeliness of Venus but, rather, portrayed the ferocity and vigor of Mars. And there is a third argument: if we wish to find some part of the lyric that corresponds to the plot in epics and tragedies, it would be no other than the ideas; for just as feelings and life-styles[78] in the former depend upon the plot, so in the lyric they depend upon the ideas. Therefore, just as, in epics and trage-dies, spirit and form inhere in the plot, we shall likewise say that in lyric poems, the ideas are the form.

Ancient rhetoricians of merit believed that as soon as an idea arises, there arises along with it a natural propriety of words and rhythms with which it is to be clothed. If this is so, how could it ever be that that idea could rightly appear dressed in another form? As Demetrius of Phalerum remarked, one could never make Love appear as one of the infernal Furies through the power of diction.[79] The quality of the words may well enhance or diminish the appearance of an idea, but it cannot totally change it—for every style of speech arises from two sources, which are the ideas and the diction (if we leave rhythm out for the moment); and there can be no doubt that the power of the ideas, such as those from which the form of speech arises, is greater than the power of diction. It is certainly the case that when the ideas differ in quality from the words and the diction, the same impropriety occurs as would occur if a peasant were dressed in the toga of a senator.

Thus, to avoid this impropriety, whoever chooses to treat important ideas in a sonnet must not clothe those ideas in low diction, as even Dante has done; for once he has given a sonnet an important subject, he must exclude all lesser concerns from it. Contrary to what has been stated—that style depends on ideas—some say that if this were the case, it would follow that when the lyric poet treated the same subjects as the epic poet (e.g., God, heroes, and the like), the style would be the same for both. But, obviously, this opinion is repugnant to truth and is thus false, etc. [*sic*]. Also, given that both treat the same subjects, it can be maintained that diction alone remains to distinguish the one sort of poetry from the other by genre and, therefore, that style derives from diction and not from the ideas.

145

But we respond to all this that there is an extremely great difference between things, ideas, and words: things are outside our minds and consist in themselves; ideas are images of things that we form in our minds in various manners according to our differing capacities to imagine; words, ultimately, are the images of images—that is, they represent to our minds by means of hearing the ideas that are drawn from things. Thus, if someone should say that style derives from ideas and ideas are the same for heroic and lyric poetry and that therefore the style of both of them is the same, I would deny that both treat the same ideas even though they both treat the same subjects sometimes.

The subject matter of the lyric is not limited. Just as the orator expands on any subject proposed to him by using probable reasons drawn from commonplaces, the lyric poet likewise treats whatever subject occurs to him.[80] However, he treats it with ideas that are his alone and do not belong to tragic and epic poets; and the difference in style between the epic and the lyric poet derives from this difference in their ideas. It is not true that what constitutes the genre of lyric poetry is sweetness of rhythm, choice of words, loveliness and splendor of diction, pictures from metaphors and other figures; rather, it is the suavity and the loveliness and, if you will, the amenity of the ideas. On the latter qualities the former depend. And there appears in these latter qualities something that is radiant, flourishing, and wanton and that is inappropriate in a heroic poem but natural in a lyric. For example, look how the epic poet and the lyric poet use different ideas when they treat the same things. From this difference in ideas derives the difference in style that we observe between them. Virgil describes for us the beauty of a woman in the person of Dido:

Regina ad templum, forma pulcherrima Dido,
incessit magna iuvenum stipante caterva.
Qualis in Eurotae ripis aut per iuga Cinthi
exercet Diana choros.
(*Aeneid* 1.496–99)

The queen paced toward the temple in her beauty,
Dido, with a throng of men behind.
As on Eurotas bank or Cynthus ridge
Diana trains her dancers.

146

DISCOURSES ON THE ART OF POETRY

This is the simplest of ideas: *forma pulcherrima Dido*. The others have somewhat more ornamentation, but not so much that they exceed the decorum of heroic poetry. However, if Petrarch as a lyric poet had to describe this same beauty, he would not have remained content with such purity in the ideas. He would have said that the earth laughs round about her; that it glories in being touched by her feet; that the grass and the flowers desire her to tread upon them; that, struck by her rays, the sky is inflamed with chastity; that it delights in becoming clear because of her glance; that the sun is mirrored in her face since it can find its peer nowhere else. The poet would invite love to join him so that together they could contemplate her glory. And the difference in style would depend on this difference in the ideas that the lyric poet would use. The epic poet would never have used ideas like those which the the lyric poet uses to his great praise:

> Qual fior cadea su 'l lembo,
> qual su le trecce bionde,
> ch'oro forbito e perle
> eran quel dì a vederle;
> qual si posava in terra, e qual su l'onde;
> qual con un vago errore
> girando parea dir: "Qui regna Amore."
> (Petrarch, *Rime* 126.46–52)

One flower fell on her skirt, another on her blond tresses, which, to see them that day, were burnished gold and pearls; another lay on the ground, another on the water, another, turning about with a lovely drifting, seemed to say: "Love rules here."

Thus, Ariosto is taken to task for using ideas in his *Furioso*, which are too lyrical:

> Amor che m'arde il cor, fa questo vento, etc.
> (23.127.5)

Love, which burns my heart, causes this wind, etc.

147

But let us make a comparison and see how the Tuscan lyric poet [Petrarch], who is perhaps superior to any Latin lyric poet, and the Latin epic poet, who is superior to all others, wrote about the same subjects. Describing the dress of Venus in the guise of a huntress, Virgil says,

> Dederatque comam diffundere ventis.
> *(Aeneid* 1.319)

> And she had given her hair
> To the disheveling wind.

He did not say that which the majesty of heroic poetry perhaps did not permit and which the lyric poet added with great loveliness:

> Erano i capei d'oro all'aura sparsi
> ch'in mille dolci nodi, etc.
> (Petrarch, *Rime* 90.1–2)

> Her golden hair was loose in the wind, which twisted it into a thousand sweet knots, etc.

Epic can allow this verse:

> ambrosiaeque comae divinum vertice odorem
> spiravere.
> (Virgil, *Aeneid* 1.403–4)

> Her ambrosial hair exhaled divine perfume from her head.

But the following would have been too wanton:

> E tutto 'l ciel, cantando il suo bel nome,
> sparser di rose i pargoletti Amori.
> (Bembo, *Rime* 12.3–4)

> And baby cupids, singing her name, sprinkle the whole sky with roses

Describing Dido when she is in love and always has her mind fixed on her beloved Aeneas, Virgil says:

148

Illum absens absentem auditque videtque.
(Aeneid 4.83)

She heard him still, though absent—heard and saw
him.

This is certainly incisive and serious, but it is simple. Petrarch, on the same subject, finds ideas that are less serious but lovelier and more ornamental; the arrangement of the words, therefore, is more picturesque and more intricate:

Io l'ho più volte (or chi fia che me 'l creda?)
nell'acqua chiara e sopra l'erba verde
veduta viva, e nel troncon d'un faggio,
e 'n bianca nube sì fatta che Leda
avria ben detto che sua figlia perde,
come stella che 'l sol coprì co 'l raggio.
(Rime 129.40–45)

Many times have I—who is there now who will believe me?— seen her alive in the clear water, and on the green grass, and in the trunk of a beech tree, and in a white cloud, in such a way that Leda would have said that her daughter was eclipsed like a star that the sun covers with its beam.

And we see that similar ideas on the same subject fill up the entire *canzone*:

In quella parte dove Amor mi sprona.
(Rime 127)

Toward where Love spurs me.

Virgil describes the lament of Dido with ordinary ideas, and therefore the words are also common:

Sic effata, sinum lachrimis implevit obortis.
(Aeneid 4.30)

Thus she spoke, and filled her bosom with her welling tears.

149

In the twelfth book he seeks much greater ornamentation in ideas when he describes Lavinia's lament, and he enlarges upon it with greater ornamentation in his words:

Accepit vocem lachrimis Lavinia matris
flagrantes perfusa genas, cui plurimus ignem
subiecit rubor et calefacta per ora cucurrit.
Indum sanguineo veluti violaverit ostro
si quis ebur vel mixta rubent ubi lilia multa
alba rosa; tales virgo dabat ore colores.
(Aeneid 12.64–69)

Lavinia, listening to her mother, streamed,
With tears on burning cheeks; a deepening blush
Brought out a fiery glow on her hot face.
As when one puts a stain of crimson dye
On ivory of India, or when
White lilies blush, infused with crimson roses,
So rich the contrast in her coloring seemed.

These are intricate ideas, and they are very close to lyric poetry: but they are not so much so that the following are not still more radiant:

perle e rose vermiglie, ove l'accolto
dolor formava voci ardenti e belle;
fiamma i sospir, le lagrime cristallo.
(Petrarch, Rime 157.12–14)

pearls and vermillion roses where the accumulated grief shaped fervent and lovely words: her sighs were flames, her tears crystal.

And Virgil might not have allowed those last verses, nor these:

Amor, senno, valor, pietade e doglia
facean piangendo un più dolce concento
d'ogni altro che nel mondo udir sì soglia;
ed era il cielo all'armonia si intento
che non si vedea in ramo mover foglia,
tanta dolcezza avea pien l'aere e 'l vento.
(Petrarch, Rime 156.9–14)

Love, wisdom, worth, piety, and sorrow—all weeping together—created a sweeter concord than any other which the world is accustomed to hear. And heaven was so intent on this harmony that not a leaf was seen moving on a branch: the air and the wind were filled with so much sweetness.

When Virgil describes the breaking of the dawn, his ideas are extremely simple:

Humentes Aurora polo dimoverat umbras;
(*Aeneid* 3.589)

Dawn had dispelled from the sky the dewy shades.

and:

Oceanum interea surgens Aurora reliquit.
(*Aeneid* 4.129)

Dawn arose meanwhile and left the ocean.

When Petrarch describes the same thing, he aims for every amenity in his ideas, and he finds words just like his ideas:

Il cantar novo e 'l pianger de gli augelli
in su 'l dì fanno risentir le valli,
e 'l mormorar di liquidi cristalli
giù per lucidi, freschi rivi e snelli.
    Quella, etc.
(*Rime* 219.1–4)

The new singing and the weeping of the birds at daybreak make the valleys echo, as does the murmur of crystal water down through the clear, fresh, quick-running brooks.

Therefore, it is apparent that differences in style derive from differences in ideas, which vary in lyric and in epic poetry and which are explained in various ways. No one may conclude that different styles do not derive from the ideas just because, when they treat the same subject, the styles nonetheless differ; for as we explained above, it does not hold that when one deals with the same subject, one deals with the same ideas. One can

151

readily treat the same subject with various ideas. And so that
the truth of all this may become more apparent, note how epic
style becomes entirely lyrical when it treats lyrical ideas. (I have
not yet decided whether or not the epic should do so.) Look
how pleasant, lovely, and intricate Ariosto is when he says,

> Era il bel viso suo, qual esser suole, . . .
> *(Orlando furioso* 11.65.1)

> Her beautiful face was as [the spring sky] when . . .

together with what follows. When a style employs such pleasant
ideas, it becomes so lyrical that one could not desire it more so.
Likewise, note how Virgil, when he uses sweet and entirely pleasant ideas, vests them in lovely diction; there results a middle and
intricate style. Read the description of the night in book 4:

> Nox erat, et placidum, etc.
> *(Aeneid* 4.522)

> Night had come and . . .

Petrarch deals with the same subject using the same sort of
ideas—that is, pleasant ones—in that sonnet:

> Or che 'l cielo e la terra e 'l vento tace.
> *(Rime* 164.1)

> Now heaven and earth and the wind were still.

Since there is no dissimilarity in the ideas there is no dissimilarity in the style. Thus, we may gather that if the lyric poet and the
epic poet were to treat the same subject with the same ideas, the
style of both would, as a result, be the same.

The style, therefore, arises from the ideas; and the ideas
likewise give rise to the quality of the verse—that is, whether it
is serious or low, etc. Virgil proves this point, since he makes
the same poetic line low, middle, and magnificent by the variation of his ideas; for if the quality of the verse determined the

ideas, Virgil would have treated pastoral themes in the magnificent style, since he used hexameter verse, which is by nature suited for serious matters. Nor is it a problem that the lyric poet sometimes uses the magnificant manner of speech and the epic poet sometimes uses the middle and the low; for the dominant quality always establishes the definition of a thing, which primarily focuses on its main intention. Thus, although the epic poet sometimes uses the middle style, we must not for this reason claim that his style is not magnificent; for the magnificent style prevails in him. And without further discussion, we shall be able to say the same thing about the lyric poet.

Tasso's Allegory of
Gerusalemme liberata

Heroic poetry, like a living creature in which two natures are joined, is composed of imitation and allegory. With the former it entices the minds[1] and the ears of men and marvelously delights them; with the latter it instructs them in either virtue or knowledge, or in both. Just as epic imitation is never anything other than a similitude and image of human action, so allegory in epic poems is customarily a figuring of human life.

Imitation focuses upon human actions that are subject to the external senses and, concentrating mainly upon these actions, tries to represent them with words that are effective, expressive, and suitable to put the things represented clearly before our corporeal eyes. Imitation does not consider the customs or feelings or discourses of the mind inasmuch as they are internal but only so far as they appear outwardly and accompany action, revealing themselves in speech and gesture and deed.

Allegory, on the other hand, regards passions and opinions and customs not only inasmuch as they are apparent but mainly in their inner essence; and it represents them obscurely with what we may call mysterious symbols, which can fully be understood only by connoisseurs of the nature of things. Now, leaving imitation aside, I shall speak of allegory, which is our present subject.

Because life is double, allegory is usually a figure of one or the other side of life; for we ordinarily understand for *man* this composite of body and soul and mind; and *human life* therefore means a life that is proper to such a composite, in whose actions each part of it concurs and by whose actions it attains that perfection of which it is naturally capable. Sometimes, though rarely, we do not understand for *man* this composite but, rather, the noblest part of it, that is, the mind; and according to this last definition we say that human life is for contemplation and purely intellectual activity, although such a life seems greatly to take part in the divine and to become angelic by almost transcending human nature.[2] Now Dante's *Comedia* [*sic*][3] is a figuring of the life of the contemplative man, as is the *Odyssey* in almost all of its parts; but we see the civic life represented throughout the *Iliad*—and in the *Aeneid*, as well, though therein we see, rather, a mixture of action and contemplation. But the contemplative man is solitary, and the active man lives in civic company. Thus it is that Dante, as well as Ulysses in taking leave of Calypso, are depicted as solitary, not as accompanied by an army or by a multitude of followers, whereas Agamemnon is portrayed as the general of the Greek army, and Achilles as the leader of many bands of Myrmidons. And Aeneas appears in company when he fights and when he undertakes other civic actions; but when he descends to the underworld and the Elysian Fields, he leaves his companions and none remains except faithful Achates, who usually never departs from his side. Not by chance does the poet imagine him going alone, for in his journey is figured one of his meditations upon the punishments and the rewards that are reserved in the otherworld for the good and evil souls. Moreover, the operation of the speculative intellect (which is the operation of a single faculty) is aptly represented by the action of a single man. However, political activity (which proceeds from the intellect, as well as from the other faculties of the mind united like citizens in a republic) can be appropriately figured forth by an action in which many come together and work toward a single end. Attending to these reasons and these examples, I formed the allegory of my poem as it will now be demonstrated.

The army, composed of various princes and other Christian soldiers, signifies mature man, who is composed of body and soul—not of a simple soul but of one distinguished by many varied faculties. Jerusalem—a strong city, located in a rough and mountainous region, toward which all the efforts of the faithful army are directed as toward an ultimate goal—signifies civic happiness, but the sort befitting a Christian, as will be clarified hereafter. This happiness is a good very hard to pursue, for it is set upon the summit of the steep and wearying ridge of virtue; and toward it, as toward an ultimate goal, are directed all the actions of political man.

Goffredo, who is captain of all this assemblage, stands for the intellect and, in particular, for that intellect which considers not necessary things but things that are mutable and can occur in various ways. He is elected captain of the enterprise through God's will and that of the princes; for the intellect is created, by God and by nature, lord over the other faculties of the soul and over the body, commanding the former by civil power and the latter by imperial rule.

Rinaldo, Tancredi, and the other princes stand for the other faculties of the soul; and the body is represented for us by the less noble soldiers. Because of the imperfection of human nature and the deceptions of its adversary, man does not attain this happiness without many internal struggles and without finding many external impediments along the way; and all of these are represented by poetic figuration. The death of Sveno and his companions—who, not having reached the camp, are slain far from it—can show us how civic man undergoes the loss of friends and followers and other external goods which are the instruments of virtue and aids in pursuing happiness. The armies of Africa and Asia and the lost battles are nothing other than the enemies and disasters and accidents of adverse fortune.

But let us come to the internal impediments: the love that causes Tancredi and the other knights to act foolishly and alienates them from Goffredo and the wrath that causes Rinaldo to stray from the enterprise. These signify the combat with the rational faculty waged by the concupiscible and the irascible faculty and the rebellion of these two. The demons that confer to prevent the conquest of Jerusalem are both figure and figured at the same time, and they represent their own selves to us in opposing our civic happiness so that it may not be our means of ascent to Christian beatitude. The two sorcerers, Ismeno and Armida, ministers of the Devil who strive to keep the Christians

157

from fighting, are two diabolic temptations that lie in wait for the two faculties of our soul from which all sins proceed. Ismeno signifies that temptation which tries to deceive what we may call the opinionative faculty with false beliefs. Armida is the temptation that lays traps for the appetitive faculty. Thus, from the former proceed the errors of opinion, from the latter, those of appetite. Ismeno's enchantments in the forest, which deceive with false imaginings, signify nothing other than the falsity of arguments and persuasions that is generated in the "forest," that is, in the multitude and variety of human opinions and discourses. The enchantment and delusion is double, since man both follows vice and flees virtue, either thinking that the hardships and dangers are too severe and insupportable or deeming (as did Epicurus and his followers) that happiness is found in pleasures and idleness. The fire, the whirlwind, the gloom, the monsters, and other such apparitions are deceptive arguments that show us honest labors and honorable dangers under the aspect of evil. The flowers, the fountains, the brooks, the musical instruments, the nymphs are false syllogisms that place before us the ease and pleasures of the senses under the aspect of good. But enough has been said of the impediments that man finds both inside and outside himself; for if the allegory of some things has not been explained, with this introduction each reader will be able to investigate it on his own.

Now let us turn to the external and internal aids by which civic man overcomes every obstacle and brings himself to the desired happiness. The diamond shield that protects Raimondo and then appears ready to defend Goffredo must be understood as the special custody of the Lord God. The angels sometimes signify divine assistance and sometimes divine inspiration, which is also suggested by Goffredo's dream and by Peter the Hermit's messages. But the Hermit, who directs the two messengers to the Sage in order to set Rinaldo free, represents supernatural understanding received through divine grace, just as the Sage represents human wisdom. For justice, temperance, contempt for death and things mortal, magnanimity, and every other moral virtue are born and grow strong through human wisdom and the understanding of nature's works and her lessons. Civic

158

man can receive great help from contemplation in each of his activities. The Sage is represented as having been pagan by birth but as having become Christian when converted by the Hermit to the true faith; and having put aside his initial arrogance, he does not presume much upon his own knowledge but defers to his Master's judgment; for philosophy was born and bred among the Gentiles [i.e., pagans] of Egypt and Greece, and from there came to us—presumptuous of her self and misbelieving, immeasurably bold and prideful. But she has been made a disciple and minister of theology by Saint Thomas and the other holy doctors; and having become more humble and devout through their efforts, she does not rashly dare to affirm anything contrary to what is revealed by her teacher. Even though Rinaldo is found and returned through the Hermit's advice alone, the figure of this sage is not introduced in vain. He is introduced to show that the grace of the Lord God does not always operate directly in men, nor through extraordianry means; rather, it often works through natural means.

Also, it is quite reasonable that Goffredo—who exceeds all others in piety and religion and who stands for the intellect, as we have said—should be especially favored and entitled to gifts of grace granted to no one else. This human wisdom, then, directed by superior virtue, frees the sensitive soul from vice and introduces moral virtue therein. But since this is not enough, Peter the Hermit hears the confessions of Rinaldo and Goffredo; and, earlier, he had reformed Tancredi.

However, since Goffredo and Rinaldo are the two characters who occupy the principal place in the poem, it perhaps will not displease the readers if I repeat some things previously stated and show in detail the allegorical sense hidden beneath the veil of their actions. Goffredo, who holds the primary place in the story, stands for nothing else in the allegory than the intellect, which is indicated in some of the poem's passages like this verse:

Tu il senno sol, tu lo scettro adopra.
(7.62.7)

You only exercise judgment, you only wield the scepter.

And more clearly in that other:

L'anima tua, mente del campo e vita.
(11.22.7)

Your soul, the mind of the camp and its life—

and *life* is added because the less noble faculties are contained in the nobler ones. Likewise, Rinaldo, who in the action is in the second degree of honor, must also be ranked in the corresponding degree in the allegory. I shall now explain what this faculty of the soul is that holds the second degree of dignity.

Among all the other faculties of the soul, the irascible is the least remote from the nobility of the mind; thus, it seems that Plato wondered whether or not it was different from reason.[4] It exists in the soul the way soldiers exist in human society. Just as it is their duty to fight against enemies in obedience to princes who have the art and knowledge of command, so the irascible faculty, as the robust and martial part of the soul, is obliged to arm itself on behalf of reason against the concupiscent faculties and, with that vehemence and ferocity characteristic of itself, to beat back and drive away everything that can be an impediment to happiness. But when this faculty disobeys reason and lets itself be carried away by its own violence, it sometimes happens that it fights not against concupiscence but on its behalf; or, like a bad watchdog, it bites the flock, rather than robbers. Although this impetuous faculty, violent and invincible, cannot entirely be figured by a single knight, it is nonetheless principally represented by Rinaldo, as is well indicated in that verse which speaks of him:

Sdegno guerrier della ragion feroce
(16.34.4)

Anger, fierce warrior of reason.

When Rinaldo exceeds the bounds of civic vengeance in fighting against Gernando or when he puts himself in the service of Armida, he can represent to us wrath ungoverned by reason;

160

when he disenchants the forest, subdues the city, routs the hostile army, he can represent wrath controlled by reason. Thus, Rinaldo's return and his reconciliation with Goffredo signifies nothing other than the obedience that the irascible faculty renders to the rational. In these reconciliations there are two noteworthy items. First, that Goffredo shows himself Rinaldo's superior with civil temperance, which teaches us that reason commands wrath not like a king but like a fellow citizen; on the other hand, Goffredo imprisons Argillano imperiously and suppresses the rebellion to help us to see that the power of the mind over the body is regal and lordly. The second item worth noting is this: the rational faculty must not exclude the irascible from action (for the Stoics were much deceived in this regard) and must not usurp its functions (since such a usurpation would be counter to natural justice) but must become its attendant and minister. Therefore, Goffredo should not himself undertake the adventure of the forest, nor should he take upon himself the other responsibilities of Rinaldo. The poet, then, would have demonstrated less art and have had less regard to that utility—which, as a subordinate to political man, he should have as his goal—if he would have represented that Goffredo alone had done all that was necessary to subdue Jerusalem.

What has been said, proposing Rinaldo and Goffredo as symbols of the irascible and rational faculties, is not contrary to, or different from, what Ugone says in the dream when he compares one to the head and the other to the right hand; for if we believe Plato, the head is the seat of reason; and the right hand, if not the seat of wrath, is at least its principal instrument.

But to come at last to the conclusion. The army in which Rinaldo and all the other knights, through the grace of God and human understanding, are returned and become obedient to the captain, signifies man brought back to the state of natural justice, when the superior faculties rule as they should and the inferior ones obey. Further, once man is in a state of divine obedience, the wood is then easily disenchanted, the city subdued, and the hostile army routed; that is, once all the external impediments are easily overcome, man achieves political happiness. But since this civic beatitude must not be the ultimate goal

161

of Christian man, he must, rather, look higher toward Christian happiness. Therefore, Goffredo does not desire to subdue the earthly Jerusalem simply to have temporal dominion over it but so that holy rites can be celebrated there and the Sepulcher freely visited by pious and devout pilgrims. And the poem closes with Goffredo's adoration to show us that the intellect, wearied in civic actions, must finally rest in prayers and contemplation of the goods of the other most blessed and immortal life.

Notes

Preface

1. Tasso, *Discourses on the Heroic Poem.*
2. See Baldassarri, "Ancora sulla cronologia dei *Discorsi dell'arte poetica*," for a recent attempt to bring some precision to the uncertain date of Tasso's early treatise.
3. Tasso, *Le lettere di Torquato Tasso*, 88–89. Luigi Poma remarks that the early *Discorsi* bear just such a relation to the *Liberata* in his edition of *Discorsi dell'arte poetica e del poema eroico*, 266.
4. Tasso, *Le lettere di Torquato Tasso*, edited by Cesare Guasti (Florence, 1852), is the most recent effort of this sort. Ettore Mazzali's one-volume edition, *Prose* (Milan, 1959), contains an annotated selection of Tasso's letters, including several from 1575–76.
5. This problem arises in Michael Murrin's use of the letters to support his argument for the authority of Tasso's allegory as a guide to reading the *Liberata* (*The Allegorical Epic*, 87–127). I address this issue in "From Aristotle to Allegory." It should also be noted that the selection of letters in the 1587 volume is entitled "Lettere poetiche," a label frequently applied to Tasso's entire *epistolario* of 1575–76. This mistaken attribution can lead readers of Tasso's letters to overlook the editorial self-fashioning at work in the original publication of *Discorsi dell'arte poetica* together with its companion pieces from Tasso's correspondence.
6. I have followed Poma's edition of *Discorsi dell'arte poetica* (Bari, 1964) in my translation; and I also have regularly consulted Mazzali's annotated edition, *Prose.* For the preface to *Rinaldo* I have used the version in Michael Sherberg's recent edition of that poem (Ravenna, 1990), and for Tasso's "Allegoria" of the *Liberata*

I have used the version in *Le prose diverse di Torquato Tasso* (Florence, 1875), edited by Cesare Guasti.

Authority and Tradition

1. Wimsatt and Beardsley, "The Intentional Fallacy."
2. See p. 98.
3. Castiglione, *Il libro del cortigiano* 1.26–7. The Latin sentence means that true art consists in hiding artifice. In the corresponding sections of his translation of *The Courtier*, Singleton renders relevant statements of this opinion. "Therefore we may call that true art which does not seem to be art," p. 43. "Such nonchalance is affected, is unbecoming, and results in the opposite of the desired effect, which is to conceal art," pp. 44–45.
4. Javitch, *Proclaiming a Classic*.
5. Hathaway, *Marvels and Commonplaces*, 179.
6. Weinberg, *A History of Literary Criticism in the Italian Renaissance*, vol. 1, pp. 424–77.
7. In *The Fusion of Horatian and Aristotelian Literary Criticism, 1531–1555*, Marvin Herrick details the process inscribed in his book's title. Tasso himself expresses a preference for a middle-of-the-road position in regard to Aristotle and Ariosto in his preface to *Rinaldo* (see pp. 96–97).
8. Tasso, *Le lettere di Torquato Tasso*, 166, n. 4. See also Tasso, *Prose*, 785, n. 3; Pittorru, *Torquato Tasso*, 122.
9. Giraldi elaborates on his problems with Pigna in a letter to Bernardo Tasso dated June 12, 1556, contained in *Delle lettere di M. Bernardo Tasso*, vol. 2, p. 196.
10. Aristotle, *Poetics* 7.1450B-51A. See p. 114.
11. See p. 123.
12. I am influenced here by Harry Berger's idea of "conspicuous allusion" in Spenser (*Revisionary Play*, 245). Also, Richard Helgerson's idea of "laureate self-fashioning" makes itself felt in what follows (*Self-Crowned Laureates*, 25, 55–100), as does Daniel Javitch's article, "Sixteenth-Century Commentaries on Imitations in the *Orlando furioso*" (pp. 221–50).
13. See p. 116.
14. Beni, *Comparazione di Omero, Virgilio e Torquato*, 154–55.
15. In the later *Discorsi*, Tasso includes discussions of the problems with Achilles as an epic hero when he inquires whether love is a

suitable theme for such poetry and when he addresses the issue of
decorum (*Discorsi dell'arte poetica e del poema eroico*, pp. 103–8,
154–60).

16. In fact, Tasso's presentation of the embassy to Goffredo involves a
    reprise of an encounter previously described in Livy 21.18 and in
    Silius Italicus' *Punica* 2.382–89.
17. See n. 7.
18. Tasso, *Le lettere di Torquato Tasso*, 136.
19. Bowra, *From Virgil to Milton*, 187–88.
20. Here, as elsewhere in this essay, I follow Lanfranco Caretti's text
    of *Gerusalemme liberata* (Turin, 1971) and Ralph Nash's transla-
    tion, *Jerusalem Delivered*.
21. Stephens, "St. Paul Among the Amazons," 173–75, 193–200.
22. Tasso, *Le lettere di Torquato Tasso*, 104–5.
23. For a discussion of formal realism, see Watt, *The Rise of the Novel*,
    9–34.
24. See p. 105.
25. Tasso often refers to Antoniano as "Il Poetino" in *Le lettere di
    Torquato Tasso* (e.g. pp. 135, 167, 173, 176 and 79, n. 2), a sobriquet
    that conveys skepticism about his literary acumen if not contempt
    for his role as a reader at this stage in the *Liberata*'s composition.
    Reference to his "soverchia severità" (p. 133) indicates how annoy-
    ing Tasso must have found Antoniano's criticism. This irritating prig
    was included among the *revisori* as a strategy to avoid intervention
    by the Inquisition in the publication of Tasso's poem, as becomes
    clear in the *Le lettere di Torquato Tasso* (e.g. pp. 128, 133–34).
    Tasso's expressions of concern about censorship elsewhere in the *Le
    lettere di Torquato Tasso* (e.g. pp. 67, 70) give a further index of how
    such apprehensions may have motivated some of his decisions.
26. It is the need for "marvels" in epic as mandated by Aristotle (*Poet-
    ics* 24.1460A) that raises this issue for Tasso; and Christianity,
    since it is, from his perspective, "true religion," enables the poet to
    reconcile the demand for such occurrences with the equally essen-
    tial requirement of verisimilitude. In the first discourse he writes,
    "Those poems where Gentile [i.e., pagan] deities are introduced
    lack this method of joining the verisimilar with the wondrous,
    whereas those poets who base their poetry on our religion can
    readily take advantage of it. In my judgment, this argument alone
    proves that the subject of an epic must be taken from Christian and
    Hebrew history, not from Gentile history." See p. 104.
27. See my "Tasso's First Discourse on the Art of Poetry as a Guide to

the *Gerusalemme liberata*," 76–80, for fuller discussion of this difference between Tasso and Trissino.

28. Milton is Tasso's true inheritor in this regard. Because they are invocations/prayers, the proems to books 1, 3, and 7 of *Paradise Lost* involve a direct transaction between the poet and the deity. Thus, they locate this religious crisis, which derives from the explicit imitation of classical form, directly and repeatedly in the foreground of Milton's epic. The opening of the *Liberata* shows Tasso's grappling with identical issues in a far more tentative manner than does his Protestant descendant.

29. "Queste medesime [opere], se si avrà riguardo a la virtù ed a la potenza di chi l'ha operate, verisimili saranno giudicate, perché, *avendo gli uomini bevuta nelle fasce insieme co 'l latte questa opinione* . . . non parrà loro fuori del verisimile quello che credono non solo esser possibile, ma stimano spesse fiate esser avvenuto e poter di nuovo molte volte avvenire" (emphasis mine). See pp. 103–4.

30. Lucretius, *De rerum natura* 1.936–42; Castiglione, *Il libro del cortegiano* 4.10; B. Tasso, *L'Amadigi* 51.1.

31. I quote from Methuen's Arden edition of Shakespeare's *As You Like It* (London, 1975), edited by Agnes Latham.

32. Here, as elsewhere in this book, I follow Hirtzel's *Virgili opera* (Oxford, 1900). For passages of more than a line or two, I follow Robert Fitzgerald's translation of the *Aeneid*. Constraints of versification make it inevitable that this English version will not match up line for line with the original; however, given his ambition to create genuinely poetic equivalents of Virgil's artistry, Fitzgerald does manage to maintain a remarkable fidelity to the Latin of the *Aeneid*. In briefer citations I make silent emendations to Fitzgerald's English or simply supply prose translations.

33. See note 24.

34. Quint, "Tasso's Clorinda"; this material will appear in his *Epic and Empire*.

35. Boiardo, *Orlando innamorato* 1.18.29–19.17.

36. Nash's footnote to his translation of these lines makes this point precisely: "In the midst of this effective passage, Tasso does not neglect to point out that this is an Aristotelian scene of recognition accompanied by peripety."

37. Javitch, "Sixteenth-Century Commentaries on Imitations in the *Orlando Furioso*."

38. In "Il Malpiglio overo della corte," Tasso's surrogate, the Neapoli-

tan Stranger, pays lavish tribute to the durability of Castiglione's guide to conduct at court: "The beauty of Castiglione's writing should make it read and praised in every age; while courts last, while princes, ladies, and knights assemble, and while courage and courtesy dwell in our souls, his name will be prized" (p. 155).

39. See p. 119.

40. Nash's translation loses the metaphorical value of this term from weaving, which specifically indicates the setting of the warp threads through which the *filo della trama*, or woof thread, is then woven. Tasso's phrase for plot structure, *testura della favola*, or weave of the tale, derives from this same lexical family of terms.

41. "Boiardo's *Orlando innamorato* wants this condition of wholeness; nor does one find it in the *Furioso* of Ariosto. The *Innamorato* lacks an ending, and the *Furioso,* a beginning. . . . Perhaps, to one who would consider the *Innamorato* and the *Furioso* as a single poem, its length could seem excessive and unlikely to be retained by an average memory after simply one reading." See pp. 115, 117.

42. Aristotle, *Poetics* 24.1460A.

43. See pp. 96–97.

44. "I concede that which I think true and which many would deny, that is, that the aim of poetry is delight. Likewise, I concede what experience shows, that is, that the *Furioso* gives people of our time greater delight than the *Italia liberata* or even the *Iliad* or the *Odyssey*." See p. 129.

   Tasso's previous and more famous comparison of Trissino and Ariosto also warrants citation in this regard. It appears when Tasso is first introducing the crucial topic of unity of plot, which he is still addressing when he makes the quoted "concession" about delight as the aim of poetry. See pp. 117–18.

45. See pp. 130–31.

46. Albert Ascoli records this curious fact in *Ariosto's Bitter Harmony*, 296, n.67.

47. See p. 137.

48. Tasso makes this point in that context with particular reference to the proems in the *Furioso*; in doing so, he asserts his agreement with Pigna that "Ariosto would not have fashioned such proems if he had not thought that, dealing with various knights and actions and often abandoning one subject and picking up another again, it was sometimes necessary to appease his audience, which is almost always done in those proems by proposing what ought to be consid-

ered in the canto and by joining those things which are to be said with those that have already been said." See p. 98.

49.

Perocché in questo loro troncar le cose, conducono il lettore a tal termine, prima che le tronchino, che gli lasciano nell'animo un ardente desiderio di tornare a ritrovarla: il che è cagione che tutto il poema loro sia letto, rimanendo sempre le principali materie imperfette insino al compimento dell'opera. (G. G. Giraldi Cinzio, *Discorso intorno al comporre dei romanzi*, 68)

For when they break off their story, they lead the reader to such a point, before they break things off, that they leave in his mind an ardent desire to return to take up the story again. This is the reason that their entire poem is read, since the principal matters always remain unfinished until the completion of the work.

50. Here, as elsewhere in this book, I follow Lanfranco Caretti's text of *Orlando furioso* (Turin, 1971) and Guido Waldman's translation, *Orlando Furioso*.
51. Daniel Javitch makes this point in "Cantus Interruptus."
52. See Bruscagli, *Stagione della civiltà estense*. The chapter on Tasso, "Il campo cristiano nella *Liberata*," contains much useful discussion of Tasso's strategies to establish and maintain a geographical center for his narrative.
53. See p. 101. Compare Joseph Conrad's similar ambition, which he records in the preface to *The Nigger of the "Narcissus"*: "My task which I am trying to achieve is, by the power of the written word, to make you hear, to make you feel—it is, before all, to make you *see*! That—and no more: and it is everything!" (p. 147).
54. Compare C. S. Lewis' remarks about "the difficult process by which Europe became conscious of fiction as an activity distinct from history on the one hand and from lying on the other" (*English Literature in the Sixteenth Century*, 318).
55. See, e.g., Watt, *The Rise of the Novel*; McKeon, "The Politics of Discourse and the Rise of the Aesthetic in Seventeenth-Century England." *The Origins of the English Novel, 1600–1740*, McKeon's impressive attempt to supersede Watt's estimable volume, is notably silent about Tasso and Ariosto, though it contains a chapter on Cervantes and reaches back as far as Greek romance and the twelfth-century "renaissance" to find "precursors" for the genre and period whose evolution it seeks to trace.
56. Gilman, *The Novel According to Cervantes*, 50, 156–64. For a

famous instance of "Ariostan" interruption, see Cervantes, *Don Quixote* 1.8–9.

57. Cervantes, *Don Quixote* 1.47–48. Cf. Forcione, *Cervantes, Aristotle, and the "Persiles"* for discussion of Cervantes' debts to Tasso and of the Don's arguments with the Canon of Toledo.

58. See, e.g., Ascoli's discussion of Cassandra's veil (*Ariosto's Bitter Harmony*, 376–93).

59. Daniel Javitch makes the point about the opening in the vernacular canon (*Proclaiming a Classic*, 14–15), and his claim accurately reflects sixteenth-century opinion such as Giovan Battista Pigna's in *I romanzi*, which he cites: "Nella nostra lingua un luogo vi era non ancora occupato" ("In our tongue there was a place that had not yet been taken" ibid., 40). In his "Introduzione ai *Discorsi dell'arte poetica* del Tasso," Guido Baldassarri remarks upon the paucity of theorizing about epic in the *Poetics*, a document primarily addressed to tragic drama (pp. 7–8).

60. 1 Corinthians 13:1; Jerome, *Select Letters of St. Jerome*, no. 22, to Eustochium. Petrarch's reference to Jerome's dilemma indicates its persistence ("On His Own Ignorance and That of Many Others," 113–14).

61. For example, Walter Kaiser thus comments on a significant omission from his study of Panurge, Stultitia, and Falstaff: "There is one important fool who might have been added to this triad, and that is Ariosto's Orlando" (*Praisers of Folly*, 15). See also Ferroni, "L'Ariosto e la concezione umanistica della follia"; Ascoli, *Ariosto's Bitter Harmony*, 259–393.

62. Cf. Ariosto, *Cinque canti* 3.21–22, in his *Opere minori*, for a subsequent example of Ariostan irony in this regard.

63. Erasmus, *"The Praise of Folly" and Other Writings*, 5–6, 242. In the quoted phrase I follow H. H. Hudson's translation, *The Praise of Folly*, 3.

64. Luther's preface to his translation of the epistle of James, for example, airs his suspicions of its rightful belonging in the sacred text; and he trims the Old Testament down to the the twenty-four books of the traditional Hebrew bible for his vernacular version, decisively excluding the Roman "deuterocanon" of the Apocrypha. Moreover, it is worth noting that when Luther summons the courage to address the German nobility, he assumes the persona of the fool, explicitly reminiscent of Stultitia in Erasmus' *Praise of Folly*. See Luther, *Martin Luther: Selections from His Writings*, 35–36, 404.

65. Dickens, *The Counter-Reformation*, 119.

66. See the "Decree concerning the edition and use of sacred books," in Council of Trent, *The Canons and Decrees of the Council of Trent*, 18.
67. Derla, "Sull'allegoria della *Gerusalemme liberata*"; Murrin, *The Allegorical Epic*, 87–127, 232–42; Olini, "Dalle direzioni di lettura alla revisione del testo."
68. I addressed this problem in my essay, "From Aristotle to Allegory."
69. "I shall pass over, for the moment, the poet's need to attend closely to improvement—if not inasmuch as he is a poet (for, as a poet, this is not his purpose), at least inasmuch as he is a citizen." See pp. 104–5. Later, in this first discourse, Tasso asserts that epics "did not originate to move either terror or pity," thus distinguishing that genre from tragedy; and he proceeds to specify the sorts of illustrious persons and deeds that would evoke wonder and awe in an audience as being appropriate for epic. See p. 108.
70. Erasmus, *"The Praise of Folly" and Other Writings*, 67–69. It seems odd to call this stinging indictment of moral hypocrisy an exposé of how certain signs lack referential value. Such oddness, however, suggests the improbability that Erasmus' own rhetorical self-defense received a favorable hearing outside the circle of sophisticated humanists who prized verbal facility for its own sake. Folly's fateful diatribe promptly transcended self-reference and was understood to refer to common grievances.
71. In designating an apt time frame in which to locate a heroic subject, Tasso writes, "Histories of times neither very modern nor very ancient do not entail the annoyance of outmoded customs nor deprive us of freedom for invention. Such are the times of Charlemagne and Arthur and those which either preceded them or succeeded them by a little; and thus it happens that they have supplied innumerable romancers with subjects for poetic composition." See p. 106. This passage also demonstrates a notable paradox in young Tasso's reckoning with the Ariostan tradition. While belonging to a larger argument that enables Tasso to expose the shortcomings of his estimable predecessor, the rationale here presented allows the aspirant access to the same subject matter as that of the *Furioso*.
72. Like Ruggiero's interlude upon Alcina's isle, the lunar episode has attracted an exceptional amount of critical attention; for these two sites in the *Furioso* provide the most detached perspectives upon the poem and thus invite global considerations. David Quint's section on Ariosto in the Tasso chapter of *Origin and Originality in*

Renaissance Literature (pp. 81–132, 235–41) has been particularly helpful to me, as has Albert Ascoli's discussion of this ascent in *Ariosto's Bitter Harmony*. The latter contains some responses to the original version of Quint's article on Astolfo's excursion that have especially influenced my reading.

73. Nearly contemporaneous experiences of visual artists provide a further index of the spirit of Tasso's age. He was bringing the *Liberata* to its initial conclusion about the time that Paolo Veronese was summoned before the Inquisition for the inclusion of "buffons, drunkards, dwarfs, Germans, and similar vulgarities" in his *Feast of the House of Levi*. During the decade when Tasso was first formulating his theories about the treatment of Christian subjects in epic poetry, Michelangelo came under the most famous and sustained of such attacks for both the indecency of naked bodies and the heresy of figures from pagan mythology in his *Last Judgment*. The first, pirated edition of the *Liberata* appeared two years before Michelangelo's follower, Bartolommeo Amannati, felt prompted to regret the nudity of statues he had carved and to wish to make public his repentance. This internalization of such rigorous codes of censorship is reminiscent of Tasso's voluntary self-submissions to the Inquisitor. See Blunt, *Artistic Theory in Italy, 1450–1600*, 114–21; Hartt, *History of Italian Renaissance Art*, 631.

Romancing the Word

1. Lewalski, *Protestant Poetics and the Seventeenth-Century Religious Lyric* 3–144, 429–56.
2. Nashe, *"The Unfortunate Traveller" and Other Works* 282–83.
3. Tasso's culture shared a kindred concern about biblical exegesis, as the Tridentine "Decree concerning the edition and use of the sacred books" evinces in its expressed wish "to repress that boldness whereby the words and sentences of the Holy Scriptures are turned and twisted to all kinds of profane usages" (Council of Trent, *The Canons and Decrees of the Council of Trent* 20). However, by attaching exegetical legitimacy to ecclesiatical authority, the Counter-Reformation church made an effort to control the biblical text's disturbing possibilities just as Tasso tried to avoid such dangers by eschewing biblical subjects as narrative sources. See Jedin, *A History of the Council of Trent*, vol. 2, 52–98. Richard Bancroft's ser-

mon, from which I quote on p. 66, addresses a similar crisis in Spenser's England that could not be as readily contained by such institutional and poetic strategies once the Reformation had gathered momentum and the break with Rome was decisively made.

4. All references to *The Faerie Queene* are to the edition of Thomas P. Roche, Jr. (New York, 1978).

5. Spenser, *Spenser: Poetical Works*, 628.

6. Cf. Josephine Waters Bennett, *The Evolution of "The Faerie Queene"*, which suggests two "Ariostan" phases in Spenser's composition of the first edition of his epic.

7. In 1587 Tasso published, together with the *Discorsi dell'arte poetica*, a selection of his letters written in 1575–76 and a few later ones, which is known as the "Lettere poetiche." The principles behind the choices that he made for that volume warrant investigation. My point here is that he had no intention to publish all of the letters of 1575–76, which are sometimes mistakenly called the "Lettere poetiche"; for they occasionally contradict one another or at least put into doubt the impression of a consistent perspective. See p. 163, n. 5

8. See Olini, "Dalle direzioni di lettura alla revisione del testo," for an account of the development of Tasso's thought on these matters after the completion of the *Liberata*.

9. Cf. Greenblatt, *Renaissance Self-Fashioning: More to Shakespeare*, 74–114, 268–76.

10. Bacon, *Novum organum* 1.129 (p. 118 in *The "New Organon" and Related Writings*).

11. Cited in Bruce, *History of the Bible in English* 37–39.

12. *The Geneva Bible*, Facsimile of the 1560 edition (Madison, 1969).

13. Bancroft, "A Sermon Preached at Paules Cross," 33–41. Robert Weimann first drew my attention to this text, which is discussed by Millar Maclure in *The Paul's Cross Sermons, 1534–1642*, 72–75. Maclure characterizes this sermon as "the major riposte by the Establishment" to the Marprelate tracts and also makes reference to the anonymous counterattacks upon Martin by Lodge and Nashe.

14. Shakespeare, *1 Henry IV* 1.2.88.

15. Nashe, *"The Unfortunate Traveller" and Other Works*, 281.

16. "Spenser shares the breadth of Lucretius' metaphysical vision and is able to make the hymn his own. But from the particular perspective of this study, he appears in the hymn as a poet whose loyalty to his own medieval roots limits his room for poetic maneuver, as one unconcerned with the exercise of bridging a rupture and playing

with the differences between the separated worlds" (Greene, *The Light in Troy*, 273–74). Again, "We cannot think of Spenser as even trying to achieve a lucid modern historicist view of Virgil, or of antiquity in general" (Kermode, *The Classic*, 61).

17. Helgerson, "The New Poet Presents Himself," in his *Self-Crowned Laureates*, is the seminal article in this trend.
18. See Nelson, *The Poetry of Edmund Spenser*, 117.
19. Greenblatt, *Renaissance Self-Fashioning*, 173–4.
20. Knapp, "Error as a Means of Empire in *The Faerie Queene* I." On the other hand, Patricia Parker's reading of Spenser in *Inescapable Romance* is suggestively akin to my approach here.
21. I allude here to John N. King's labeling Spenser and his circle "progessive Protestants" in "Was Spenser a Puritan?" and to Wallace MacCaffrey's distinction between *politiques* and idealists in *Queen Elizabeth and the Making of Policy, 1572–1588*.
22. Cauchi, "The 'Setting Foorth' of Harrington's Ariosto"; Javitch, *Proclaiming a Classic*.
23. See p. 167, n. 39
24. Cf. Durling, "The Bower of Bliss and Armida's Palace"; Judith Kates, *Tasso and Milton*, 136–44.
25. Greenblatt, *Renaissance Self-Fashioning*, 179.
26. Lewis, *The Allegory of Love*, 332.
27. See p. 167, n. 39
28. All citations are from the text as it appears in *John Milton: Complete Poems and Major Prose*, edited by Merritt Y. Hughes (New York, 1957).

Milton's Change of Note

1. E.g., in "The Reason of Church Government Urged Against the Prelaty," "Of Education," and "The Second Defense of the People of England," in *John Milton: Complete Poems and Major Prose*, 637, 668, 829.
2. See pp. 97–98.
3. Lewalski, *"Paradise Lost" and the Rhetoric of Literary Forms*, 36–38, 220.
4. See pp. 107–8.
5. See p. 98.
6. Cf. canto 35, where Saint John the Evangelist exposes the power of patrons to "call the tune" of dependent poets and thus to "revise"

history. The worldly ironies of his lunar discourse correspond to
the tonal hints cited here from the proem to canto 3. In canto 35
fulsome praise of the Estensi is resumed, only to be pointedly
juxtaposed to a series of allegedly fraudulent tributes by Homer,
Virgil, and Saint John himself. These acknowledged misrepresenta-
tions indict Ariosto's prior celebration of his sponsors via guilt by
association and suggest that he, too, may merely be paying lip
service to his patron's house in hopes of a generous reward.

7. "When the poet speaks in his own person, he is allowed to think
and speak as though with a different mind and a different tongue
and much beyond ordinary usage, because we believe him inspired
and rapt with divine *furor*." See p. 137.

8. Wittreich twice employs Tasso's famous purple passage about
variety-in-unity and *discordia concors*, which first appeared in
Discorsi dell'arte poetica, in order to assimilate Tasso's idea of the
epic as an all-inclusive genre to the encyclopedic comprehensive-
ness of prophetic discourse (" 'A Poet Amongst Poets,' " 130;
idem, *Visionary Poetics*, 11–12). I discuss some of the issues that
this connection raises in my essay, "After the Middle Ages."

9. See pp. 135–36.

10. Milton, *John Milton: Complete Poems and Major Prose*, 637, 668.

11. See p. 105.

12. In this regard a rare instance of Milton's tonal affinity with Ariosto
warrants mention—the Paradise of Fools in *Paradise Lost* 3.418–
97, which derives from the lunar dumping ground in canto 35 of
the *Orlando furioso*. Milton strikes his own distinctive note in this
reprise, but his debt to Ariosto in the comic aspect of this passage
deserves consideration.

13. Steadman, "*Paradise Lost* and the Tragic Illustrious," 302.

14. Johnson, *Lives of the English Poets*, vol. 1, 103.

15. Blake, plate 5 of *The Marriage of Heaven and Hell*, in *The Complete Poetry and Prose of William Blake*.

16. Fish, *Surprised by Sin*, 1–22.

17. Daniel Javitch makes some apposite comments in this regard in
"Narrative Discontinuity in the *Orlando furioso* and Its Sixteenth-
Century Critics," 73–74.

18. Goethe, *Torquato Tasso*; Byron, "The Lament of Tasso" in *The
Poetical Works of Byron*, vol. 5, 77–93. Baudelaire, "Sur le Tasse
en Prison," in his *Fleurs du Mal*, 193–94.

19. Montaigne, *The Complete Essays*, 363.

20. See p. 131.

21. Ferguson, *Trials of Desire*, 212, n. 22.
22. Scrutiny of this passage can dissociate it further from the context of Oedipus, since the patricide in question is described as "voluntary." This discrepancy indicates how applications of theories of the unconscious sometimes seem awkwardly ad hoc in the pursuit of their preordained conclusions. See pp. 99–100.
23. Ferguson, *Trials of Desire*, 59–60.
24. Tasso, *Le lettere di Torquato Tasso*.
25. Hampton, *Writing from History*, 124, n. 52.

Torquato Tasso to His Readers

1. This brief preface accompanied the text of *Rinaldo* (1562). I follow the version in Michael Sherberg's edition of the poem.
2. Tasso's term here, *ordir*, derives from the lexicon of weaving and specifies the lengthwise arrangement of the warp threads, across which the woof thread (*filo della trama*) is drawn at right angles. The language of this craft frequently serves as a resource for discussions of narrative *dispositio*. See p. 167, n. 40
3. Tasso here plays a Ciceronian ideal of corporeal wholeness off against the Aristotelian value of unity of plot; and he gains, in the process, room for himself to maneuver as a "modern romancer." See Aristotle, *Poetics* 8.1451a and Cicero, *Tusculan Disputations* 4.13.31. Michael Sherberg discusses this passage and makes these connections in "The Sign of Transition."

Discourses on the Art of Poetry

1. In discussing how to write a heroic poem, Tasso employs three stages in the composition of a speech according to classical rhetoric: invention, disposition, and elocution. Though the three discourses that follow clearly fit these headings, some ambiguity arises at the close of the second discourse and raises the question of a missing discourse. See p. 178, n. 43 about this problem.
2. Aristotle, *Poetics* 14.1453B.
3. Tasso here evokes the rhetorical concept of *enargeia* (clarity or vividness), "which makes us seem not so much to narrate as to exhibit the actual scene," according to Quintilian, *Institutio oratoria* 6.2.32.
4. Aristotle, *Poetics* 9.1451B.

5. In Virgil's *Aeneid* 9.77–125, ships turn into nymphs. The other marvels occur regularly in romance.
6. Tasso addresses the *Discorsi* to his patron and friend, Scipione Gonzaga.
7. Aristotle, *Poetics* 1.1447A.
8. Ibid. 9.1451B.
9. Tasso's phrase *la testura della favola*, which I render as "plot structure," may be more tellingly construed as the "weave of the tale," if one wishes to capture the root meaning of the first noun and something of the traditional discourse about narrative prior to the mid cinquecento that remains operative in the early *Discorsi*. For example, images drawn from weaving recur in Ariosto's asides about his advancing story. See *Orlando furioso* 13.80–81.2 and the discussion on pp. 41–42. Tasso's participation in the decisive emergence of a new school of literary theory should not obscure his inevitable debt to earlier understandings of narrative technique and should not project him as a structuralist *avant la lettre*.
10. Aristotle, *Poetics* 1.1447A.
11. Ibid. 4.1449B, 9.1452A.
12. Ibid. 13.1453A.
13. Tasso mentions a character from each of the great classical epics, as well as Amadis, who appears in Bernardo Tasso's *L'Amadigi*, and Bradamante, who appears in Ludovico Ariosto's *Orlando furioso*.
14. Mezentius in Virgil's *Aeneid* 10.689–908; Marganorre in Ariosto's *Orlando furioso* 37.42–121; Archeloro in B. Tasso's *L'Amadigi*, *passim*, esp. 30; Busiris, mythical king of Egypt, who sacrificed strangers to Jupiter; Procrustes, the famous torturer, who was killed by Theseus; and Diomedes, king of Thrace, who fed his horses on human flesh and was killed by Hercules.
15. Florio is the hero of Boccaccio's *Filocolo*; Theagenes and Characlea are the heroes of Heliodorus' *Aethiopica*.
16. Aristotle, *Poetics* 6.1449B-50A.
17. Lucan's *Pharsalia* and Silius Italicus' *Punica*.
18. Sperone Speroni was an author and a professor of philosophy at Padua, where Tasso regularly visited his home during the years 1560–62.
19. Actually, Plato taught in the Academy, and Aristotle in the Lyceum.
20. Tasso's distinction between subject matter (*materia nuda*) and the form of the plot (*favola*) reproduces the ancient rhetorical categories of *inventio* and *dispositio*. It is worth noting, however, their striking resemblance to such structuralist categories as *histoire* and *récit*.

21. Aristotle, *Poetics* 7.1450B-51A.
22. Tasso cites these lines in Italian. In the early *Discorsi* there are no citations in Greek; there are many in the revised and expanded version of 1594.
23. Tibullus, *Carmina* 1.3.75.
24. Petrarch, *Triumphus famae* 3.102 in his *Rime, trionfi e poesie latine*.
25. "And each defends himself with his own great authority" (Lucan, *Pharsalia* 1.127). The text actually reads, "Magno se iudice."
26. Aristotle, *Poetics* 9.1451B.
27. Horace, *Ars poetica* 23. In Latin the text, which Tasso renders in Italian, reads, "Denique sit quidvis, simplex dumtaxat et unum."
28. Tasso again misquotes slightly. The text reads,"Si volet usus / quem penes arbitrium est et ius et norma loquendi."
29. Tasso's word here is *specifica*, which is best rendered "generic"; however, one loses, in the process, the relationship between generic distinctions, on the one hand, and accidental and essential differences, on the other, which is the basic premise of Tasso's line of argument at this point. For Tasso, in this context, distinctions between genres are essential differences; yet he lacks a term like "mode" to indicate those of less consequence (accidental) though nonetheless requiring discrimination.

    Besides quibbling over a liberty taken in the translation, it is worth noting at this juncture the general instability of the idea of genre in the emerging neoclassicism of Tasso and other theorists in the second half of the sixteenth century. The generic identity of epic and romance is the major theme of young Tasso's second discourse and, arguably, of the early *Discorsi* in their entirety; for it enables Tasso to counter Pigna and Giraldi, the defenders of Ariosto, without totally disinheriting himself from that line of popular poetry. Thus, his appeal to the idea of genre is crucial, even though that idea itself is unstable.
30. Aristotle, *Poetics* 1.447A.
31. Tasso left the hiatus in this passage, which he did not complete. He is drawing his terms from the brief fragment by Aelius Donatus, *Excerpta de comoedia* 6.1.19–21 in *Commentus Terenti*. Scaliger cites this passage from Donatus and expands upon it in *Poetices libri septem* 1.7.
32. "A complete brief art," that is, the *Poetics*.
33. Guasti cites Aulus Gellius, *Noctes Atticae* 1.10 as the source of this statement, in his edition, *Le lettere di Torquato Tasso*.

34. M. Curius Dentatus refused the gold of the Samnites. In *Annales* 12 Ennius wrote of him, "Quem nemo ferro potuit superare nec auro." Cicero quotes this verse in *De republica* 3.3.6. In Petrarch's *Triumphus famae* 2.30 (in his *Rime, trionfi e poesie latine*), Cimon would have suffered his own incarceration if his father, Miltiades, who died in prison, had been denied proper burial.
35. Cicero, *Tusculan Disputations* 4.13.31.
36. This is the poet son of Frederick II, who was captured by the Bolognese Guelfs in 1249 and died in captivity in 1272. Tasso uses his name to make general reference to the poets of Frederick's court.
37. Homer, *Odyssey* 6.
38. "This is the task, this the toil" (Virgil, *Aeneid* 6.129).
39. Aristotle, *Poetics* 10.
40. Ibid. 11.
41. Ibid. 18.1455B–56A.
42. Ibid. 24.
43. Since Tasso proceeds to speak of diction, not of variety, it is possible that one of the early discourses is missing. This possibility increases when we note that Tasso twice refers to his early poetics as containing *four* books: first, in a letter to Ercole Rondinelli in 1570 (*Le lettere di Torquato Tasso*, 22); second, at the very beginning of his *Discorsi del poema eroico* (1594). He does keep the promise made here in the third of those later discourses.
44. Tasso's main source in this discourse is the treatise *On Style* mistakenly attributed to Demetrius of Phalerum. He knew it via the Latin translation and commentary of Pietro Vettori, *Commentarii in librum Demetri Phalerei* (Florence, 1562).
45. A slight misquote. Line 5 should read, "Ma, a dire il vero, esso v'avea la gola." For this and other such corrections, I follow Lanfranco Caretti's edition of the poem (Turin, 1971).
46. The text in Ariosto reads, "A un uom; e tuttavia; basse l'ale." The translation includes the missing lines (3–4) in order to make better sense of the passage in English.
47. Demetrius (attr.), *On Style* 2.38.
48. Ibid. 2.75.
49. Ibid. 2.122–27.
50. Ibid. 5.265.
51. Ibid. 2.77.
52. Aristotle, *Poetics* 20.1456B. Tasso here distinguishes between words or parts of words that have a functional, rather than a con-

ceptual, value. Thus, a letter, a syllable, an article has no meaning per se; and the last of these would be a "simple" word composed of "no meaningful element."

53. Ibid. 21.1457B.
54. Dante's text reads, "Che paia."
55. No source for this quote has been found.
56. Ennius coined this word (*Annales* 2, frag. 18).
57. Demetrius (attr.), *On Style* 2.77.
58. Ibid. 2.83–84.
59. Ibid. 2.89.
60. Ibid. 2.44–47.
61. Ibid. 5.247.
62. Quoting from memory, Tasso again slightly errs. The verse should read, "Tu fanciullo e veloce. . . ."
63. Demetrius (attr.), *On Style* 2.115.
64. Ibid. 2.116.
65. Ibid. 2.118–119.
66. Ibid. 2.122–27.
67. Ibid. 4.190.
68. Dante's line actually reads, "Poi è Cleopatràs lussuriosa."
69. Demetrius (attr.), *On Style* 3.128–56.
70. Ibid. 3.186–89.
71. Ibid. 4.209–22. The principle here expressed is that of *enargeia* (clarity or vividness), which Tasso also invoked in the first discourse. Cf. p. 175.
72. Demetrius (attr.), *On Style* 4.217.
73. The line should read, "Guardommi un poco. . . ."
74. Dante, *Inferno* 33.4–75.
75. This verse cannot be located in Ariosto or elsewhere.
76. Dante, *De vulgari eloquentia* 2.4, 7.
77. Aristotle, *Rhetoric* 3.2.5–6. See pp. 137–38, where Tasso appeals to a kindred Aristotelian notion. "Ideas are no more than images of things. Unlike things, these images have no real or solid substance in themselves; but they have a certain imperfect being in our minds, and thence they are shaped and formed by the imagination."
78. This modern expression captures what critics nowadays term the "socially constructed" aspect of character, or ethos—the rhetorical concept that Tasso's *costumi* points to in this passage.
79. Demetrius (attr.), *On Style* 3.132.
80. This is an ancient idea: see Cicero, *De oratore* 1.16.70.

Tasso's Allegory of *Gerusalemme liberata*

1. Tasso here writes *animi*; but since elsewhere in the "Allegoria" he maintains no stable distinction between *animo* and *anima* as rational and spiritual faculties respectively, I have not tried to force one upon his text. As he employs them, the terms seem generally interchangeable; and I have chosen the English word that seems best in each instance.
2. Tasso here employs Dante's famous coinage in *Paradiso* 1.70 when he attempts to explain the insufficiency of language to describe his ascent from the Mount of Purgatory to Paradise.
3. Tasso's spelling perhaps reflects Dante's reference to his own poem by this name in *Inferno* 16.128, although this form carries a grave accent in most texts.
4. Plato, *Republic* 4.440.

Bibliography

Primary Sources

Ariosto, Ludovico. *Opere minori*. Ed. Cesare Segre. Milan: Ricciardi, 1964.

――――. *Orlando furioso*. Ed. Lanfranco Caretti. Turin: Einaudi, 1971.

――――. *Orlando Furioso*. Trans. Guido Waldman. New York: Oxford University Press, 1983.

Aristotle. *The "Art" of Rhetoric*. Trans. John Henry Freese. Loeb Classical Library, 193. Cambridge: Harvard University Press, 1959.

――――. *The Poetics*. Trans. W. Hamilton Fyfe. In *Aristotle*, XXIII. Loeb Classical Library, 199. Cambridge: Harvard University Press, 1982.

Bacon, Francis. *The "New Organon" and Related Writings*. Ed. Fulton H. Anderson. New York: Macmillan, 1960.

Bancroft, Richard. *Sermon Preached at Paules Cross*. London: G. Seton, 1588/9. STC 1346.

Baudelaire, Charles. *Les Fleurs du Mal*. Paris: Garnier Frères, 1961.

Beni, Paoli. *Comparazione di Omero, Virgilio, e Torquato*.In *Opere di Torquato Tasso colle controversie sulla "Gerusalemme,"* vol. 21, ed. Giorgio Rossi. Pisa: Capurro, 1828.

Blake, William. *The Complete Poetry and Prose of William Blake*. Ed. David V. Erdman. Berkeley: University of California Press, 1982.

Boiardo, Matteo Maria. *Orlando innamorato*. 2d ed. Ed. Aldo Scaglione. 2 vols. Turin: Unione Tipografico-Editrice Torinese, 1963.

Byron, George Gordon. *The Poetical Works of Byron*, vol. 5. Boston: Little, Brown, 1851.

Castiglione, Baldesar. *The Book of the Courtier*. Trans. Charles S. Singleton. New York: Doubleday, 1959.

———. *Il libro del cortigiano*. 3d. ed. Ed. Vittorio Cian. Florence: Sansone, 1929.

Cervantes, Miguel de. *Don Quixote*. Trans. J. M. Cohen. New York: Penguin, 1950.

Cicero, Marcus Tullius. *De oratore*. Trans. E. W. Sutton. Loeb Classical Library, 348–49. Cambridge: Harvard University Press, 1942.

———. *De republica*. Trans. Clinton Walker Keyes. Loeb Classical Library, 213. Cambridge: Harvard University Press, 1951.

———. *Tusculan Disputations*. Trans. J. E. King. Loeb Classical Library, 141. Cambridge: Harvard University Press, 1971.

Conrad, Joseph. *The Nigger of the "Narcissus."* Ed. Robert Kimbrough. New York: Norton, 1979.

Council of Trent. *The Canons and Decrees of the Council of Trent*. Trans. H. J. Schroeder and O. P. Rockford, IL: Thomas A. Nelson Books and Publishers, 1978.

Dante Alighieri. *De vulgari eloquentia*. Ed. Pier Vincenzo Mengaldo. Padova: Antenore, 1968.

———. *Divina Commedia*. Rev. ed. Ed. C. H. Grandgent. Boston: Heath, 1933.

Demetrius (attr.). *On Style*. Trans. W. Rhys Roberts. In *Aristotle*, XXIII. Loeb Classical Library, 199. Cambridge: Harvard University Press, 1982.

Donatus, Aelius. *Commentum Terenti*. Ed. Paul Wessner. Leipzig: B. G. Teubner, 1902.

Ennius, Caecilius. *Annales*. Trans. E. H. Warmington. In *Remains of Old Latin*, I. Loeb Classical Library, 294. Cambridge: Harvard University Press, 1961.

Erasmus, Desiderius. *"The Praise of Folly" and Other Writings*. Ed. Robert M. Adams. New York: Norton, 1989.

———. *The Praise of Folly*. Trans. H. H. Hudson. Princeton: Princeton University Press, 1941.

The Geneva Bible. A facsimile of the 1560 edition. Madison: University of Wisconsin Press, 1969.

Giraldi Cinzio, G. G. *Discorso intorno al comporre dei romanzi*. In *Scritti critici*. Ed. Camillo Guerrieri Crocetti. Milan: Mazorati, 1973.

Goethe, Johannes Wolfgang von. *Torquato Tasso*. Trans. Charles E. Passage. New York: Ungar, 1966.

Homer. *The Odyssey*. Trans. A. T. Murray. Loeb Classical Library, 104–5. Cambridge: Harvard University Press, 1919.

Horace. *Ars poetica*. Trans. H. R. Fairclough. Loeb Classical Library, 194. Cambridge: Harvard University Press, 1978.

Jerome. *Select Letters of St. Jerome*. Trans. F. A. Wright. Loeb Classical Library, 262. Cambridge: Harvard University Press, 1933.

Livy. *Livy*. Ed. B. O. Foster. Loeb Classical Library, 233. Cambridge: Harvard University Press, 1929.

Lucan. *The Civil War (Pharsalia)*. Ed. J. D. Duff. Loeb Classical Library, 220. Cambridge: Harvard University Press, 1928.

Lucretius. *De rerum natura*. Ed. W. H. D. Rouse. Loeb Classical Library, 181. Cambridge: Harvard University Press, 1924.

Luther, Martin. *Martin Luther: Selections from His Writings*. Ed. John Dillenberger. New York: Anchor, 1969.

Milton, John. *John Milton: Complete Poems and Major Prose*. Ed. Merritt Y. Hughes. New York: Odyssey, 1957.

Montaigne, Michel Eyquem de. *The Complete Essays*. Trans. Donald M. Frame. Stanford: Stanford University Press, 1957.

Nashe, Thomas. *"The Unfortunate Traveller" and Other Works*. Ed. J. B. Steane. New York: Penguin, 1972.

Petrarch, Francesco. *Canzoniere*. Ed. Gianfranco Contini. Turin: Einaudi, 1968.

———. "On His Own Ignorance and That of Many Others." In *The Renaissance Philosophy of Man*. Ed. Ernst Cassirer, Paul Oskar Kristeller, John Herman Randall, Jr. Chicago: University of Chicago Press, 1948.

———. *Rime, trionfi e poesie latine*. Ed. Ferdinando Neri, Guido Martello, Enrico Bianchi, and Natalino Sapegno. Milan: Ricciardi, 1951.

Pigna, Giovan Battista. *I romanzi*. Venice: Vicenzo V. Valgrisi, 1554.

Plato. *Republic*. Trans. Paul Shorey. Loeb Classical Library, 237–38. Cambridge: Harvard University Press, 1969.

Quintilian. *Institutio oratoria*. Trans. H. E. Butler. Loeb Classical Library, 124–28. Cambridge: Harvard University Press, 1920–22.

Scaliger, Julius Caesar. *Poetices libri septem*. A facsimile of 1561 edition. Stuttgart: Friedrich Frommann Verlag, 1964.

Shakespeare, William. *As You Like It*. Ed. Agnes Latham. London: Methuen, 1975.

———. *1 Henry IV*. Ed. A. R. Humphreys. London: Methuen, 1966.

Silius Italicus. *Punica*. Ed. J. D. Duff. Loeb Classical Library, 277–78. Cambridge: Harvard University Press, 1927–34.

Spenser, Edmund. *The Faerie Queene*. Ed. Thomas P. Roche, Jr. New York: Penguin, 1978.

———. *Spenser: Poetical Works*. Ed. J. C. Smith and E. de Selincourt. Oxford: Oxford University Press, 1970.

Tasso, Bernardo. *Delle lettere di M. Bernardo Tasso accresciute, corrette, e illustrate*. Ed. Anton-Federigo Seghezzi. 2 vols. Padova: Giuseppe Comino, 1733.

————. *L'Amadigi di Gaula*. Venice: Antonelli, 1835.

Tasso, Torquato. *Discorsi dell'arte poetica e del poema eroico*. Ed. Luigi Poma. Bari: Laterza, 1964.

————. *Discourses on the Heroic Poem*. Trans. Mariella Cavalchini and Irene Samuel. Oxford: Oxford University Press, 1973.

————. *Gerusalemme liberata*. Ed. Lanfranco Caretti. Turin: Einaudi, 1971.

————. "Il Malpiglio overo della corte." In *Tasso's Dialogues*. Trans. Carnes Lord and Dain A. Trafton. Berkeley: University of California Press, 1982.

————. *Jerusalem Delivered*. Trans. Ralph Nash. Detroit: Wayne State University Press, 1987.

————. *Le lettere di Torquato Tasso*. Ed. Cesare Guasti. Florence: Le Monnier, 1852.

————. *Le prose diverse di Torquato Tasso*. Ed. Cesare Guasti. Florence: Le Monnier, 1875.

————. *Prose*. Ed. Ettore Mazzali. Milan: Ricciardi, 1959.

————. *Rinaldo*. Ed. Michael Sherberg. Ravenna: Longo, 1990.

Tibullus. *Tibullus*. Trans. J. P. Postgate. In *Catullus, Tibullus, "Pervigilium Veneris."* Loeb Classical Library, 6. Cambridge: Harvard University Press, 1913.

Virgil. *The Aeneid*. Trans. Robert Fitzgerald. New York: Random House, 1983.

————. *Virgili opera*. Ed. Frederick A. Hirtzel. Oxford: Oxford University Press, 1900.

Secondary Sources

Ascoli, Albert. *Ariosto's Bitter Harmony: Crisis and Evasion in the Italian Renaissance*. Princeton: Princeton University Press, 1987.

Baldassarri, Guido. "Ancora sulla cronologia dei *Discorsi dell'arte poetica*." *Bergamum: Bollettino della civica biblioteca* 78 (1984): 3–4, 99–110.

————. "Introduzione ai *Discorsi dell'arte poetica* del Tasso." *Studi tassiani* 26 (1977): 5–38.

Bennett, Josephine Waters. *The Evolution of "The Faerie Queene."* New York: Franklin, 1960.

Berger, Harry. *Revisionary Play: Studies in the Spenserian Dynamics.* Berkeley: University of California, 1988.

Blunt, Anthony. *Artistic Theory in Italy, 1450–1600.* Oxford: Oxford University Press, 1940.

Bowra, C. Maurice. *From Virgil to Milton.* London: Macmillan, 1945.

Bruce, Frederick F. *History of the Bible in English.* New York: Oxford University Press, 1978.

Bruscagli, Riccardo. *Stagione della civiltà estense.* Pisa: Nitri-Lischi, 1983.

Cauchi, Simon. "The 'Setting Foorth' of Harington's Ariosto." *Studies in Bibliography* 36 (1983): 137–69.

Derla, Luigi. "Sull'allegoria della *Gerusalemme liberata.*" *Italianistica* 7 (1978): 473–88.

Dickens, Arthur G. *The Counter-Reformation.* London: Thames & Hudson, 1966.

Durling, Robert. "The Bower of Bliss and Armida's Palace." *Comparative Literature* 6 (1954): 335–47

Ferguson, Margaret W. *Trials of Desire: Renaissance Defenses of Poetry.* New Haven: Yale University Press, 1983.

Ferroni, Giulio. "L'Ariosto e la concezione umanistica della follia." In *Atti del Convegno Internazionale "Ludovico Ariosto."* Rome: Accademia Nazionale dei Lincei, 1975.

Fish, Stanley. *Surprised by Sin: The Reader in "Paradise Lost."* Berkeley: University of California Press, 1971.

Forcione, Alban K. *Cervantes, Aristotle, and the "Persiles."* Princeton: Princeton University Press, 1970.

Gilman, Stephen. *The Novel According to Cervantes.* Berkeley: University of California Press, 1989.

Greenblatt, Stephen. *Renaissance Self-Fashioning: More to Shakespeare.* Chicago: University of Chicago Press, 1980.

Greene, Thomas. *The Light in Troy: Imitation and Discovery in Renaissance Poetry.* New Haven: Yale University Press, 1982.

Hampton, Timothy. *Writing from History: The Rhetoric of Exemplarity in Renaissance Literature.* Ithaca: Cornell University Press, 1990.

Hartt, Frederick. *History of Italian Renaissance Art.* New York: Abrams, 1979.

Hathaway, Baxter. *Marvels and Commonplaces.* New York: Random House, 1968.

Helgerson, Richard. *Self-Crowned Laureates: Spenser, Jonson, Milton, and the Literary System.* Berkeley: University of California Press, 1983.

Herrick, Marvin. *The Fusion of Horatian and Aristotelian Literary Criticism, 1531–1555*. Urbana: University of Illinois Press, 1946.

Javitch, Daniel. "Cantus Interruptus." *Modern Language Notes* 95 (1980): 66–80.

―――. "Narrative Discontinuity in the *Orlando furioso* and Its Sixteenth-Century Critics." *Modern Language Notes* 103 (1988): 50–74.

―――. *Proclaiming a Classic: The Canonization of "Orlando furioso."* Princeton: Princeton University Press, 1991.

―――. "Sixteenth-Century Commentaries on Imitations in the *Orlando furioso*." *Harvard Library Bulletin* 34 (1986): 221–50.

Jedin, Hubert. *A History of the Council of Trent*. London: Nelson & Sons, 1961.

Johnson, Samuel. *Lives of the English Poets*. London: Dent & Sons, 1968.

Kaiser, Walter. *Praisers of Folly*. Cambridge: Harvard University Press, 1963.

Kates, Judith. *Tasso and Milton: The Problem of Christian Epic*. Lewisburg, PA: Bucknell University Press, 1983.

Kermode, Frank. *The Classic: Literary Images of Permanence and Change*. Cambridge: Harvard University Press, 1975.

King, John N. "Was Spenser a Puritan?" *Spenser Studies* 6 (1986): 1–31.

Knapp, Jeffrey. "Error as a Means of Empire in *The Faerie Queene* I." *English Literary History* 54 (1987): 801–34.

Lewalski, Barbara K. *Protestant Poetics and the Seventeenth-Century Religious Lyric*. Princeton: Princeton University Press, 1979.

―――. *"Paradise Lost" and the Rhetoric of Literary Forms*. Princeton: Princeton University Press, 1985.

Lewis, C. S. *The Allegory of Love: A Study in Medieval Tradition*. Oxford: Oxford University Press, 1936.

―――. *English Literature in the Sixteenth Century*. Oxford: Oxford University Press, 1954.

MacCaffrey, Wallace. *Queen Elizabeth and the Making of Policy, 1572–1588*. Princeton: Princeton University Press, 1981.

McKeon, Michael. *The Origins of the English Novel, 1600-1740*. Baltimore: Johns Hopkins University Press, 1987.

―――. "The Politics of Discourse and the Rise of the Aesthetic in Seventeenth-Century England." In *Politics of Discourse*. Ed. Kevin Sharpe and Steven N. Zwicker. Berkeley: University of California Press, 1975.

186

Maclure, Millar. *The Paul's Cross Sermons, 1534–1642*. Toronto: University of Toronto Press, 1958.

Murrin, Michael. *The Allegorical Epic*. Chicago: University of Chicago Press, 1980.

Nelson, William. *The Poetry of Edmund Spenser: A Study*. New York: Columbia University Press, 1963.

Olini, Lucia. "Dalle direzioni di lettura alla revisione del testo: Tasso tra 'Allegoria del poema' e *Giudizio.*" *La rassegna della letturatura italiana* 7 (1985).

Parker, Patricia. *Inescapable Romance: Studies in the Poetics of a Mode*. Princeton: Princeton University Press, 1979.

Pittorru, Fabio. *Torquato Tasso: L'uomo, il poeta, il cortigiano*. Milan: Bompiani, 1982.

Quint, David. *Epic and Empire*. Princeton: Princeton University Press. Forthcoming.

———. *Origin and Originality in Renaissance Literature: Versions of the Source*. New Haven: Yale University Press, 1983.

———. "Tasso's Clorinda." Presented at the meeting of the Modern Languages Association, Chicago, 1990.

Rhu, Lawrence F. "After the Middle Ages: Prophetic Authority and Human Fallibility in Renaissance Epic." In *Poetry and Prophecy*. Ed. James L. Kugel. Ithaca: Cornell University Press, 1990.

———. "From Aristotle to Allegory: Young Tasso's Evolving Vision of the *Gerusalemme liberata.*" *Italica* 65 (1988): 111–30.

———. "Tasso's First Discourse on the Art of Poetry as a Guide to the *Gerusalemme liberata.*" *Journal of the Rocky Mountain Medieval and Renaissance Association* 7 (1986): 65–81.

Sherberg, Michael. "The Sign of Transition: Notes on the Corporeal Analogy in the Early Tasso." In *Studies in Honor of Fredi Chiappelli*. Ed. Dennis Dutschke. Padova: Antenore. Forthcoming.

Steadman, John. "*Paradise Lost* and the Tragic Illustrious." *Anglia* 78 (1968): 302–16.

Stephens, Walter. "St. Paul Among the Amazons: Gender and Authority in *Gerusalemme liberata.*" In *Discourses of Authority in Medieval and Renaissance Literature*. Eds. Kevin Brownlee and Walter Stephens. Hanover: University Press of New England, 1989.

Watt, Ian. *The Rise of the Novel*. Berkeley: University of California Press, 1957.

Weinberg, Bernard. *A History of Literary Criticism in the Italian Renaissance*. 2 vols. Chicago: University of Chicago Press, 1961.

Wimsatt, W. K., and Beardsley, Monroe C. "The Intentional Fallacy."

In *The Critical Tradition*. Ed. David H. Richter. New York: St. Martins Press, 1989.

Wittreich, Joseph. " 'A Poet Amongst Poets': Milton and the Tradition of Prophecy." In *Milton and the Line of Vision*. Ed. Joseph Wittreich. Madison: University of Wisconsin Press, 1975.

————. *Visionary Poetics: Milton's Tradition and His Legacy*. San Marino, CA: Huntington Library, 1979.

Index